CW00346122

بسم الله الرحمن الرحيم

"The house of al-Arqam is the house of Islām"

Al-Ḥākim (d.405 h) in *al-Mustadrak ʿala al-Ṣaḥiḥayn* (6185)

Learning About *Īmān*

تعليم الإيمان

as-Sayyid, al-ʿAllāmah

Ṣiddīq Ḥasan Khān al-Qanūjī (1307/1890)

The *Nawāb* of Bhopal

DAR AL-ARQAM

ISBN: 978-1-8384897-7-9

British Library Cataloguing in Publishing Data
A catalogue record for this book is available from the British Library

© Copyright 2022 Dar al-Arqam

All rights reserved worldwide. No part of this publication may be reproduced in any language, stored in a retrieval system or transmitted in any form or by any means, electronic, mechanical, photocopying, recording or otherwise without the express permission of the publisher.

Prepared and published by Dar al-Arqam Publishing,
Birmingham, United Kingdom

Translated from the original Urdu by:
Abū Ubaydah Arsalān Yūnus (Ark Of Knowledge)

www.daral-arqam.co.uk
Email: daralarqam@hotmail.co.uk

If you would like to support our work, donations can be made via:

- www.daralarqam.bigcartel.com/product/donate
- www.patreon.com/daralarqam
- www.paypal.me/daralarqam

While every precaution has been taken in the preparation of this book, neither the authors and translators shall have any liability with respect to any loss or damages caused nor are the views expressed in this book necessarily held by the translator directly or indirectly by the instructions or advice contained in this book.

Learning About Īmān

al-Sayyid, al-ʿAllāmah
Nawāb Siḍḍīq Ḥasan Khān al-Bhopālī

الفهرس

Contents

Foreword

In the words of the author this small treatise is the explanation of complete *Īmān* which is the means of entering Paradise. The first thing which he mentioned at the start of this treatise is a summarised explanation of the famous ḥadīth of Jibrīl and highlighted its importance. He then goes on to mention a summarised definition of *Īmān*, its pillars, levels, the virtue of the statement of *Tawḥīd* as well as other issues pertaining to *Aqīdah* in a concise way.

This treatise was authored by him on Wednesday the 9th of Jūmādul Ākhirah in the year 1305 Hijrī. It took 2 days to complete and was published in the lifetime of the author in 34 pages.[1]

1 [TN] The author has also published other short treatises based on the pillars of Islām such as *Taʿlīmus Ṣalāh (Learning About Ṣalāh), Taʿlīmuz Zakāh (Learning About Zakāh), Taʿlīmus Ṣiyām (Learning About Ṣiyām), Taʿlīmul Ḥajj (Learning About Ḥajj)* and *Taʿlīmudh Dhikr Wad Duʿā (Learning About Dhikr and Duʿā) etc.*

Biography of the Author

His name is Siḍḍīq Ḥasan Khān al-Qanūjī al-Bhopālī al-Ḥusaynī.

Based on his family tree history, his lineage traces back to the Prophet (*Ṣallallāhū 'Alayhī Wa Sallam*) through 33 forefathers and therefore this would make him a *Sayyid*.

He was born on Sunday the 19th of Jūmādul Ula in the year 1248 Hijrī corresponding to the 14th of October 1832 at his mother's village, Banis Barele. His father Awlād Hasan was from the village of Qanūj and that is where he was taken shortly after his birth. His father studied with the likes of Shaykh Shāh 'Abdul'azīz Dehlawī (who was the son of Shāh Walīyullāh Dehlawī), Shaykh Shāh Rafī'udīn and Shaykh Shāh 'Abdulqādir Dehlawī and authored around 17 books on the topics of propagating the Qur'ān and Sunnah.

When he was 5 years old, his father passed away at the age of 43 so he was raised by his mother. When this happened Shaykh Nawāb Siḍḍīq Ḥasan Khān and his family were left in great poverty and had nothing except the books which were left behind by his respected ancestors. So he kept looking into these books and this created a great zeal and influence for him to seek knowledge. His mother highly encouraged him to learn the religion. At the age of 7, she would make sure he would always pray in the *Masjid* which was just opposite their house.

He initially studied in his own locality and with his brother Aḥmad

Ḥasan 'Arshī . After that, when he was a little older, he travelled to Fārūkhabād, Kānpur and finally to the centre of Islamic knowledge in his region, Delhi, in the year 1853 when he was 21 years old. During his studies he learned Arabic, *Fiqh*, *Tafsīr*, *Ḥadīth* and other sciences from the likes of Shāh 'Abdul'azīz Dehlawī and Shaykh 'Abdulqādir Mūḥadith Banārsī (the student of Imām Muḥammad Bin 'Alī ash-Shawkānī) etc.

After studying and obtaining knowledge of all the Islamic sciences Nawāb Siḍḍīq Ḥasan Khan returned to Qanūj as his brother Aḥmad Ḥasan 'Arshī had passed away, so he had to look for a job in order to financially support his family. Eventually he went to the state of Bhopal for employment and received a job from Jamāluddīn Ṣiddīqī Dehlawī who was the First Minister of state for Bhopal. After some years of employment, Jamāluddīn noticed Shaykh Nawāb Ṣiddīq Ḥasan Khān's excellent qualities and knowledge, so he wed Nawāb Ṣiddīq Ḥasan Khān to his widowed daughter, Zakīyah Begum in the year 1861.

The ruler of Bhopal, Sīkandar Begum passed away in the year 1868 and she was replaced by her daughter Shāhjahān Begum who was married to Nawāb Muḥammad Khān, but he died a year before. This left Shāhjahān Begum as a widow when she became the leader of the state of Bhopal, and she needed a husband to help her look after the affairs of the state. Her mother mentioned to her the qualities of Nawāb Ṣiddīq Ḥasan Khān, such as his knowledge, piety and long years of service, so she wanted to marry him and thus they married in the year 1871. Through this he would enjoy the same status as the Nawāb (Viceroy), which is a royal title indicating a sovereign ruler, and essentially acted as the head of state for Bhopal. Shāhjahān

Begum took the knowledge of the Qur'ān and Sunnah from him and she would give orders according to his views.

With his new-found authority he launched orphanages, *Masjids* and research centres for the propagation of Islamic academic works etc. He made every effort to prevent and exterminate crime in order to promote peace and security within his region. He provided incentives to those who would memorise books such as *Ṣaḥīḥ al-Bukhārī* and *Bulūghul Marām*. He spent lots of money on buying the manuscripts of *Tafsīr Ibn Kathīr*, *Fatḥul Bārī Sharḥ Ṣaḥīḥ al-Bukhārī* and *Naylul Awṭār* etc. and published them in order to distribute them for free and make them become easily available to the scholars and students of knowledge. He spent 50,000 rupees (of his era) on *Fatḥul Bārī* alone which shows that he was funding a significant amount of wealth towards these ventures. Before this, these books were not obtainable in the Indian Subcontinent. Due to all of this effort, Bhopal flourished in becoming the centre for the scholars of ḥadīth and knowledge for a certain period of time.

He authored many articles and books in Arabic, Persian and Urdu on the topics of *Tafsīr*, ḥadīth, *'Aqīdah*, *Fiqh*, *Taqlīd*, *Tarīkh*, *Akhlāq* etc. which totalled to around 230. Some of them are as follows:

- *Fatḥul Bayān Fī Maqāsid Al-Qur'ān*
- *Arba'ūna Ḥadīthan Fi Faḍā'il Al-Ḥajj Wal 'Umrāh*
- *As-Sirāj Al-Wahāj Min Kashf Maṭālib Ṣaḥīḥ Muslim Bin Al-Ḥajjāj*
- *'Awn Al-Bārī Li Hal Adillah Al-Bukhārī*

- *Fatḥul 'Allām Bī Sharh Bulūghul Marām*
- *Rawḍatan Nadīyah Sharḥ Durar Al-Bahīyah*
- *Qaṭf Athamar Fī 'Aqā'id Ahlil Athar*
- *Al-Hiṭah Fī Ḍhikr As-Ṣihāh As-Sittah*
- *Al-Balāghah Īlā Usūl Al-Lughah*
- *Riyāḍ Al-Jannah Fī Tarājim Ahlis Sunnah*
- *Iksīr Fī Usūl At-Tafsīr*
- *Misk Al-Khitām Sharh Bulūgh Al-Marām*
- *Itihāf An-Nubalā Al-Mutaqīn Bī Ihyā Mathar Al-Fuqahā Al-Muhadīthīn*
- *Sāfīyah Sharh Kāfīyah*
- *Tafsīr Tarjūmān Al-Qur'ān Bī Latāif Al-Qur'ān*
- *Bughyah Al-Qārī Fī Thulathiyat Al-Bukhārī*
- *Makārim Al-Akhlāq*
- *Tawfīq Al-Bārī Tarjamah Al-Adab Al-Mufrad Lil Bukhārī*
- *Ikhlās At-Tawḥīd Lil Ḥamīd Al-Majīd*
- *'Aqīdah As-Sunnī*
- *Ḥādī Al-Qalb As-Salīm Īlā Darajāt Janat An-Na'īm*
- *Muntakhab Zād Al-Mutaqīn Li Shaykh 'Abdul Ḥaq Ad-De-*

hlawī

Shaykh Nawāb Ṣiddīq Ḥasan Khān was recognised around the world as being a scholar of high calibre, as evidenced from the following quotes of other scholars.[2]

Shaykh Ḥusayn Bin Muḥsin Ansārī Yamāni said he was the exalted Sayyid, the honoured scholar, Sharīf from genealogy and origin. Sunnī of high eminence and standing, gathering Sharīf from both sides (father and mother), Shaykh Ṣiddīq Ḥasan.

Shaykh Jamāludīn Qāsīmī mentioned in his *Ijāzah* to Shaykh Ḥāmid Fiqhī that he was the famous *Imām*, lover of the Sunnah and its books.

Shaykh Rashīd Riḍā Miṣrī said about him that he was the author of famous books which are the pillars for the revival of knowledge and religion.[3]

Shaykh Muḥammad al-Bashīr Ibrāhīmī al-Jazā'irī counted him among the great scholars.[4]

Shaykh Shamsulḥaq 'Aẓīmabādī stated that he was among the Mujaddidīn of the beginning of the 13th century...the sublime scholar, the noble and complete *Mūḥadith*, combining abundant sciences and author of many books, Nawāb Ṣiddīq Ḥasan Khān al-Bhopālī

2 [TN] Some of them taken from Shaykh Zīyād Tuklāh's introduction to *Silsilah Asjad Fi Ḍhikr Masaykh Sanad*

3 [TN] *al-Manār* vol no.14 pg no.471

4 [TN] *Majmū' of Shaykh Muḥammad al-Bashīr Ibrāhīmī al-Jazā'irī* vol no.4 pg no.38

al-Qanūjī.[5]

He had a vast library and after he passed away it was transferred to Darul ʿUlūm Nadwatul ʿUlamā in Lakhnow.

Since he had the responsibility of being the First Minister, he would travel and go to official meetings in Delhi and Calcutta in which the viceroy and other British officials would come. Seeing the progress of the Ahlul Ḥadīth *daʿwah*, the enemies started to plot against him and invented fabrications as is the usual tactic of those who are jealous when they see someone who is successful. All of these invented fabrications have been answered numerous times in writings by himself, his family and his students which are clear for the intelligent seeker of truth to see.

Nawāb Ṣiddīq Ḥasan Khān passed away at the age of 57 (according to the Gregorian calendar) on the 29th of Jūmādul Ākhirah in the year 1307 Hijrī, corresponding to the 18th of February 1890 at 1:30am. A great number of people attended his *Janāzah*, so much so that it had to be done multiple times.[6]

5 [TN] *ʾAwnul Maʿbūd Sharḥ Sunan Abī Dāwūd* vol no.11 pg no.266
6 [TN] For a detailed account of his biography refer to books such as *40 Ahl-E-Ḥadīth Scholars From The Indian Subcontinent pg no.407 - 421*

Introduction

I begin with the name of Allāh, the Most Gracious, Most Merciful.

I testify that there is no deity worthy of being worshipped in truth except Allāh and I testify that Muḥammad is His slave and His messenger. To proceed:

This short treatise is an explanation of having complete *Īmān,* which is the means of entering Paradise. O Allāh, I ask you for Paradise, and I seek refuge with you from the Fire!

The Ḥadīth of Jibrīl Is the Basis of *Īmān*

The ḥadīth of Jibrīl has the status of forming the basis and origins on the subject of *Īmān*, which has been narrated by 'Umar Bin al-Khaṭṭāb ﷺ in *Marfū'*[7] form. He narrates that Jibrīl ﷺ came to the Prophet ﷺ and first asked him about Islam, that what is Islam?

The Prophet ﷺ said:

> Islam is that you testify that there is no deity worthy of being worshipped in truth except Allāh and bear witness that Muḥammad is His messenger, perform prayer, pay the *Zakāh*, fast in the month of Ramaḍān and perform Ḥajj to the House

7 [TN] *Marfū'* means a ḥadīth exclusively attributed to the Prophet ﷺ, *Muqaddimah Ibn Ṣalāh* pg no.27

of Allāh if you can afford it.[8]

I have mentioned these four things in separate treatises, but here the purpose is to only explain the statement about *Īmān*.

Then, in response to Jibrīl's ⚊ question, the Prophet ⚊ explained *Īmān* as:

> *Īmān* is that you believe in Allāh, in His Angels, in His books, in the Hereafter, and in the good and the bad of destiny.

Then Jibrīl ⚊ asked about *Ihsān*, to which he ⚊ replied:

> *Ihsān* is that you worship Allāh Almighty as if you see Him, and if you do not see Him, then He is looking at you.

Ihsān is mentioned in this ḥadīth, which means sincerity, and it is connected with both Islām and *Īmān*. Without *Ihsān*, an individual's Islām cannot be correct and neither can *Īmān*. This is because without it, the Islām of the individual will consist of showing off, and showing off is a type of hidden *Shirk*. Similarly, without *Ihsān*, the *Īmān* of an individual will consist of hypocrisy and the hypocrite is worse than a disbeliever.

It Is Obligatory on Every Muslim to Understand *Īmān* and Islām

It is obligatory on every Muslim to understand the meaning of *Īmān* and Islām very well. If the individual does not understand it well, then they will be a Muslim in name only, and their *Īmān* will be weak, it will not be complete.

---

8 *Saḥīḥ Muslim* ḥadīth no.8

Abū Hurayrah ﵁ narrated that the Prophet ﷺ said:

> There are around seventy odd branches and levels of *Īmān*. The best level of *Īmān* is (acknowledging and acting upon the statement or *Kalimah*) there is no deity worthy of being worshipped in truth except Allāh alone and the lowest level is to remove something harmful from the road.[9]

This ḥadīth proves that *Īmān* is a combination of words and deeds.

The Sign of Having Complete *Īmān*

The completeness of *Īmān* is that the Prophet ﷺ is considered more beloved than the father, the son and all people. It states in the ḥadīth narrated from Anas ﵁ that the Prophet ﷺ said:

> None of you can become a believer unless I become more beloved to you than your father, children and all other people.[10]

Imām al-Khaṭṭābī said:

> The meaning of this love does not mean inherent love, rather it means voluntary love which is done with one's own intention.

Imām Ibn Baṭṭal said:

> This ḥadīth means that a person who has complete *Īmān* is well aware of the fact that the right of the Prophet ﷺ is greater than the rights of the father, the son and all people."[11]

9 *Saḥīḥ al-Bukhārī* ḥadīth no.9, *Saḥīḥ Muslim* ḥadīth no.35
10 *Saḥīḥ al-Bukhārī* ḥadīth no.15, *Saḥīḥ Muslim* ḥadīth no.44
11 *Sharh Saḥīḥ Bukhārī* by Ibn Baṭṭāl vol no.1 pg no.22

Qaḍī 'Iyāḍ said:

> Indeed, the reality of *Īmān* is completed only by the domination of the love of the Prophet ﷺ. To the extent that *Īmān* is not complete without the domination of love and status of the Prophet ﷺ over the father, the son and every virtuous benefactor. On the contrary, a person who believes in something other than that is not a believer.[12]

Meaning *Īmān* is not complete without prioritising the love of the Prophet ﷺ over the love of all people.

Three Things Without Which There Is No Pleasure In *Īmān*

It is narrated on the authority of Anas ؓ that the Prophet ﷺ said:

> Whoever possesses the following three qualities will have the sweetness of *Īmān*:
>
> 1. The one to whom Allāh and His Messenger become dearer than anything else.
>
> 2. Who loves a person and he loves him only for Allāh's sake.
>
> 3. Who hates to revert to disbelief as he hates to be thrown into the fire.[13]

The Basis of Love

It is mentioned in *As-Sirāj Al-Wahhāj* that the basis of love is that

---

12 *Ikmālul Mū'alim Sharḥ Saḥīḥ Muslim* by Qaḍī 'Iyāḍ vol no.1 pg no.204
13 *Saḥīḥ al-Bukhārī* ḥadīth no.16, *Saḥīḥ Muslim* ḥadīth no.43

the heart is inclined towards the harmony of the beloved. Sometimes a person's heart is attracted to something that he loves, such as good looks, a good voice and good food. Sometimes the heart of the lover is inclined towards the inner virtues of the beloved, such as the love of scholars, pious worshippers and the people of virtue, and sometimes he loves to do good to someone and to remove harm for them. All these virtues are present in the Prophet ﷺ because he has the virtues of outward and inward beauty, perfection of morals, guidance for the servants of Allāh to the straight path and turning them away from Hell.[14]

As for the overwhelming excessive type of love that men and women have for their lovers, it is a great temptation and trial. Doctors consider this type of love to be a form of disease. In the eyes of the Sharī'ah, this type of love is *Shirk* and is against *Tawḥīd*, and in the eyes of the intellect, it is foolishness and nonsense.

Who Has Tasted *Īmān*?

A third ḥadīth is narrated from 'Abdullāh Bin 'Abbās that the Prophet ﷺ said:

"Whoever is content with Allāh being the Rabb[15], Islām being the religion and Muḥammad being the Messenger ﷺ then they have tasted *Īmān*."[16]

---

14 *As-Sirāj al-Wahhāj Min Kashf Maṭālib Saḥīḥ Muslim Bin al-Hajāj* vol no.1 pg no.136

15 [TN] The word *Rabb* has a vast meaning. Its detailed meaning is the Sustainer, Cherisher, Master and Nourisher.

16 *Saḥīḥ Muslim* ḥadīth no.34

In this ḥadīth the words "content with Allāh being the Rabb" have the following meaning:

From the word 'Allāh', *Tawḥīd Ulūhīyah*[17] is established and from the word 'Rabb', *Tawḥīd Rubūbīyah*[18] is established. By professing these a person becomes a complete believer. A person who professes only one type of *Tawḥīd* and denies the other type of *Tawḥīd* is a disbeliever or a polytheist; in any case he is not a believer. *Īmān* is valid as long as the love and affection for anyone else is not equal to Allāh and His Messenger ﷺ.

The author of *Taḥrīr has* written:

> This ḥadīth (mentioned above) means that a person who does not ask for anything from anyone other than Allāh and does not strive for anything other than the way of Islām and follows only that which is in accordance with the Sharī'ah of Muḥammad ﷺ, then whoever possesses this virtue, surely the sweetness of *Īmān* has reached his heart and he has tasted it.[19]

The Requirement of Love for Allāh and His Messenger ﷺ

Allāh says:

وَالَّذِينَ آمَنُوا أَشَدُّ حُبًّا لِّلَّهِ ﴿١٦٥﴾

{And those who believe have the most amount of love

---

17 [TN] *Tawḥīd Ulūhīyah* means believing that Allāh is unique without rival in His divinity and in worship.
18 [TN] *Tawḥīd Rubūbīyah* means believing that Allāh is unique, without partner in His dominion and His actions.
19 *Sharh Saḥīḥ Muslim by al-Nawawī* vol no.2 pg no.2

for Allāh.} [Sūrah al-Baqarah: 165]

Imām Mālik said:

> The love for Allāh and His Messenger ﷺ is one of the obligations and duties of Islām. This love requires that the human being obey Allāh and His Messenger ﷺ and renounce any opposition to them.

Therefore, whosoever receives and possesses this type of love will have no need of and will become disgusted with the stranger who is opposed to Allāh and His Messenger ﷺ.

The person who has some flaws and shortcomings in their love is a weak Muslim. They do not obtain pleasure in their *Īmān* and neither do they value or recognise the full worth of their religion.

Perseverance and Affirmation Are Essential Components of *Īmān*

There is a ḥadīth narrated from Sufyān ath-Thaqafī ﷺ that the Prophet ﷺ said:

> "Say! I believe in Allāh, and then persevere in it."[20]

The meaning of this ḥadīth is that there must be perseverance with *Īmān*, otherwise the hypocrites are also apparent believers and many believers are polytheists, as Allāh says:

وَمَا يُؤْمِنُ أَكْثَرُهُم بِاللَّهِ إِلَّا وَهُم مُّشْرِكُونَ ﴿١٠٦﴾

20 *Saḥīḥ Muslim* ḥadīth no.38

{And most of them do not believe in Allāh except that they (declare themselves to be believers in Allāh but) also commit polytheism with Him at the same time.} [Sūrah Yūsuf: 106]

Perseverance in *Īmān* is counted when a person declares the testimony of faith, acts upon it and performs four other deeds (namely *Ṣalāh*, *Ṣiyām*, Ḥajj and *Zakāh*) and confirms *Īmān* with their heart. That is why the Prophet ﷺ said in a ḥadīth, which is narrated from Ṭalhah that:

> He will have succeeded if he meant what he said and made it an actuality (that I will not underestimate the pillars of Islām and will uphold their rights).[21]

The Prophet ﷺ made the person's success conditional to their truthfulness. So if there is no truthfulness and actuality to what they say, then there is no success.

Deeds Are an Integral Part of *Īmān*

Having certainty in *Īmān* and being sincere to it means that what is confessed with the mouth should be permanent in the heart and should be practiced with the limbs and joints. That is why the Prophet ﷺ applied the word *Īmān* to the deeds of Islām in the ḥadīth of the delegation of 'Abdul Qays and declared that deeds are part of *Īmān*.[22] [Reported by al-Bukhārī]

Similarly, in a ḥadīth narrated from Abū Sa'īd Al-Khuḍrī the

21 *Saḥīḥ al-Bukhārī* ḥadīth no.46, *Saḥīḥ Muslim* ḥadīth no.11
22 *Saḥīḥ al-Bukhārī* ḥadīth no.53, *Saḥīḥ Muslim* ḥadīth no.17

Prophet ﷺ described women as having reductions in mind and religion. He ﷺ explained this by stating that the reductions of their religion is that they do not offer *Ṣalāh* and do not fast during menstruation and the reductions of their mind is that their testimony is half that of a man.[23] [Agreed upon]

From the above ḥadīth, it is known that reductions in performing deeds [sometimes] leads to defects and weakness in religion.

Īmān Is Not Static, It Increases and Decreases

It is written in the books of *Īmān* that *Īmān* increases and decreases. Just as *Īmān* increases with the increase of obedience, so does *Īmān* decrease with the decrease of obedience and the committing of sins. That is why Allāh has said in the Qur'ān that a good person and an

23 *Saḥīḥ al-Bukhārī* ḥadīth no.298, *Saḥīḥ Muslim* ḥadīth no.79. [TN] This refers to a woman's legal obligations and is not an ontological statement that women are always less in mind or religion than men. In other cases a woman's testimony is accepted in important matters of family law without any man present at all. The reductions for women are a manifestation of Islām's leniency towards women, by not burdening them with the same obligations as men. With regards to her reduction in mind, then women are not obligated to perform some functions such as testifying before a judge in a criminal case. As for her reduction in religion, women are not obligated to pray or fast while menstruating or enduring post-natal bleeding. Ibn al-Qayyim states that, "The [default position is that a] woman is equal to the man in truthfulness, honesty and piety. Otherwise, if it is feared that she will forget or misremember, she is strengthened with another like herself. That makes them stronger than a single man." (*at-Ṭuruq al-Ḥukmīyah* vol no.1 pg no.136). Ibn Taymiyyah states that, "Whatever there is among the testimonies of women, in which there is no fear of habitual error, they are not considered as half of a man." (*at-Ṭuruq al-Ḥukmīyah* vol no.1 pg no.128)

evil person are not equal. Since the one who is righteous is a complete believer, while the evil one has deficient *Īmān*.

Allāh says:

أَمْ حَسِبَ الَّذِينَ يَعْمَلُونَ السَّيِّئَاتِ أَن يَسْبِقُونَا ۚ سَاءَ مَا يَحْكُمُونَ ﴿٤﴾

> **Or do those who do evil deeds think they can outrun [i.e., escape] Us? Evil is what they judge.** [Sūrah al-ʿAnkabūt: 4]

When thousands of the evil people from the nation of Mūsā ﷺ perished from the punishment of Allāh and Mūsā ﷺ became very saddened by their sudden death, Allāh said:

فَلَا تَأْسَ عَلَى الْقَوْمِ الْفَاسِقِينَ ﴿٢٦﴾

> **{(O Mūsā!) So do not grieve for the death of these transgressors.}** [Sūrah al-Māʾidah: 26]

Since they are worthless in the sight of Allāh because their *Īmān* is not complete. If they had true love for Allāh and His Messenger ﷺ they would never have acted against His command. In particular, they would have tried to avoid committing major sins and would have avoided small, big, hidden and blatant innovations. However, their hearts are dominated by the love of someone other than Allāh, so that is why their *Īmān* is weak and lacking. This love for someone other than Allāh will be an obstacle to their salvation.

Take out whatever is in your heart except the truth,

Otherwise opposition to the truth will become an obstacle to your salvation.

Another Step Towards Complete *Īmān*

Abu Ūmāmah ﵁ narrated that the Prophet ﷺ said:

> Whoever loves someone for the sake of Allāh and dislikes someone for the sake of Allāh, gives to someone for the sake of Allāh, and if he withholds from someone, he does so for the sake of Allāh, then he has completed his *Īmān*.[24] [Reported by Abū Dāwūd and At-Tirmidhī]

Further Levels of *Īmān*

Abū Hurayrah ﵁ narrated from the Prophet ﷺ that:

> A Muslim is that individual from whose tongue and hand other Muslims are safe and a believer is that individual whereby other people may live in peace from him, with regards to their lives and property.[25] [Reported by at-Tirmidhī and an-Nasā'ī]

In the narration of Imām al-Bayhaqī there are additional words that:

> A *Mūjāhid* is the one who fights against himself (his desires) in order to stay obedient to Allāh and a *Mūhājir* is the one who abandons sins.[26]

From this, it is known that the outward appearance of performing

24 *Sunan Abī Dāwūd* ḥadīth no.4681, *Sunan at-Tirmidhī* ḥadīth no.2521
25 *Sunan at-Tirmidhī* ḥadīth no.2726, *Sunan an-Nasā'ī* ḥadith no.4995
26 *Shu'abul Īmān* vol no.7 pg no.499

the deeds of Islam is not valid, unless the intention of the doer is sincere and their heart is pure.

It is narrated in a ḥadīth that:

> Allāh does not look at your faces and your deeds, but He sees your hearts and intentions.[27]

The Heart Has Declared That, "There Is No Deity Worthy Of Worship In Truth Except Allāh." So What Do You Get?

Someone asked Wahb Bin Munabih, "Is (declaring that) there is no deity worthy of worship in truth except Allāh not the key to Paradise?" So he replied:

> Yes! But the key also has teeth. If you bring a key that has (the correct) teeth, the door to Paradise will open for you, otherwise it will not open.[28]

This means that *Īmān* is of little use without deeds.

What Is *Īmān*?

Abu Ūmāmah ﵁ narrated that a man asked the Prophet ﷺ, "What is *Īmān*?" So the Prophet ﷺ replied:

> When you like good deeds and dislike sins, then you are a be-

27 *Saḥīḥ Muslim* ḥadīth no.2564
28 [TN] This narration is mentioned in *Saḥīḥ al-Bukhārī* without any *Isnād* however it is mentioned with a full *Isnād* in *Ḥilyatul Awlīyā* of Imām Abū Naʿīm Iṣfahānī vol no.4 pg no.22. In conclusion the *Isnād* is weak, for details see *Taghlīq at-Taʿlīq* of Ibn Ḥajar vol no.2 pg no.454

liever.

Then he asked: "What is sin?" The Prophet ﷺ said:

> When something gives you a hindrance (hitch, problem) in your heart, then give it up.[29] [Reported by Aḥmad]

From the above ḥadīth it is known that a person who does not dislike sinning, then they have a defect in their *Īmān*. The Prophet ﷺ also explained and clarified what a sin is, i.e. a sin is that which causes a hindrance (hitch, problem) in your heart.

Similarly, 'Amr Bin 'Abasah ؓ asked the Prophet ﷺ "What is *Īmān*?" The Prophet replied:

> Patience and forbearance.

Meaning, to be patient in leaving off sins and to be steadfast with regards to obedience to Allāh.

He then asked: "What is the best *Īmān*?" The Prophet ﷺ said:

> Good character.[30] [Reported by Aḥmad]

The words of this ḥadīth (good character) include all the noble characteristics, both outward and inward. This has been described in detail in my book *Makārimul Akhlāq*.

The Best *Īmān*

Mū'ādh Bin Jabal ؓ asked the Prophet ﷺ about the best *Īmān*. The

29 *Musnad Aḥmad* vol no.5 pg no.252
30 *Musnad Aḥmad* vol no.4 pg no.385

Prophet ﷺ said:

> That is: your friendship and enmity should be for the sake of Allāh alone and you should always remember Allāh with your tongue.[31] [Reported by Aḥmad]

Fighting the Individual Who Testifies the Statement of *Īmān* But Does Not Perform *Ṣalāh* and Does Not Give *Zakāh*

Ibn ʿUmar ؓ narrated that the Messenger of Allāh ﷺ said:

> I have been commanded (by Allāh) to fight with the people until they testify that there is no deity worthy of worship in truth except Allāh and that Muḥammad is the Messenger of Allāh ﷺ and that they should perform the *Ṣalāh* and pay *Zakāh*. So, if they do this then they will save their lives and property from me, except when other Islamic verdicts are applicable[32], and their reckoning is with Allāh."[33] [Agreed upon]

If they do this hypocritically, Allāh will hold them accountable, however from their apparent actions they will be treated like Muslims. Since there were many hypocrites in the time of the Prophet ﷺ, the Qur'ān is full of condemnation of them.

Reasons For Entering Paradise

Abū Hurayrah ؓ narrated that a Bedouin asked the Prophet ﷺ,

---

31 *Musnad Ahmad* vol no.5 pg no.247

32 [TN] Meaning when people commit other crimes and are sentenced to punishments based on the appropriate Islamic rulings

33 *Saḥīḥ Bukhārī* ḥadīth no.25, *Saḥīḥ Muslim* ḥadīth no.22

"Tell me such a deed that when I do it, I will enter Paradise." The Prophet ﷺ said:

> Worship Allāh alone and do not associate anyone with Him. Perform the obligatory *Ṣalāh*, pay the obligatory *Zakāh* and observe the fast of Ramadhān.

On hearing this, the Bedouin said: By Him in Whose hand is my life, I will never do less than what you have stated and neither will I do more than it.

When the Bedouin started to leave, the ﷺ said:

> Whoever would like to see a person of Paradise, then let him look at that (Bedouin) person.[34] [Agreed upon]

In the above ḥadīth, entering Paradise is based on not committing polytheism and fulfilment of the obligatory Islamic duties. This ḥadīth proves that good deeds are required to enter Paradise.

A Doubt and the Answer to It

It has been narrated in a ḥadīth that the entry of Paradise will be possible only by the grace of Allāh.[35] So how can it be correct to make the entry of Paradise conditional on good deeds?

The answer to this is that although the attainment of Paradise is not based on deeds but on the grace of Allāh alone, deeds are considered as a symbol of the grace of Allāh which is that righteous deeds are the means of attaining the grace of Allāh. The entry into Paradise is

---

34 *Saḥīḥ Bukhārī* ḥadīth no.1333, *Saḥīḥ Muslim* ḥadīth no.14
35 *Saḥīḥ Bukhari* ḥadīth no.5349, *Saḥīḥ Muslim* ḥadīth no.2816

conditional on this type of grace.

In the ḥadīth about the delegation of 'Abdul Qays, the members of the delegation asked the Prophet ﷺ what it means to believe in Allāh alone. So he ﷺ said:

> Declaring that there is no deity worthy of worship in truth except Allāh alone and that Muḥammad is the Messenger of Allāh, performing the obligatory *Ṣalāh*, paying the obligatory *Zakāh* and observing the fast of Ramadhān.[36] [Agreed upon]

Additionally, this ḥadīth shows that the deeds of the religion are considered a part of *Īmān*.

Taking Allegiance on Performing Good Deeds and Leaving Disobedience

'Ubādah Bin Ṣāmit ؓ narrated that the Prophet ﷺ said to a group of his Companions:

> Swear allegiance to me that you will not associate anything in worship with Allāh, do not steal, do not commit adultery, do not kill your children, do not slander and do not disobey me in any matter. Whoever of you fulfils this pledge, his reward is established with Allāh, and whoever commits any of these deeds, then he will be punished for it in this world (in accordance to the Sharī'ah compliant verdicts). Then that punishment will become the expiation of that sin for him. Whoever does any of these deeds, then Allāh conceals his sin, then it is up to Allāh whether He forgives him or punishes him.

---

36 *Saḥīḥ Bukhārī* ḥadīth no.53, *Saḥīḥ Muslim* ḥadīth no.17

(The Companion states that) "We swore allegiance to the Prophet ﷺ on this."[37] [Agreed upon]

There is good news in this ḥadīth that whoever is covered up for his sins, he will be forgiven *inshā Allāh*.

The Importance and Virtue of Avoiding *Shirk*

The Messenger ﷺ once said to Mū'ādh ؓ:

> Do you know what is the right of Allāh on His servants and the right of the servants over Allāh?

Mū'ādh ؓ replied, "Only Allāh and His Messenger ﷺ know best."

He ﷺ said:

> It is the right of Allāh over the servants that they should worship Allāh alone and not associate anything in worship with Him, and the right of Allāh's servants is that whoever does not associate anything in worship with Allāh, then Allāh will not punish them.

On hearing this, Mū'ādh ؓ asked, "O Messenger of Allāh ﷺ, shouldn't I tell people the good news?"

He ﷺ said:

> Do not give them these glad tidings, lest they sit back and become complacent and rely on this only.[38]

---

37 *Saḥīḥ Bukhari* ḥadīth no.3679, 6787, *Saḥīḥ Muslim* ḥadīth no.1709
38 *Saḥīḥ Bukhārī* ḥadīth no.2701, *Saḥīḥ Muslim* ḥadīth no.30

That is, it shouldn't be the case where people end up becoming complacent and relying on this good news and therefore do not perform any deeds.

According to another narration, the Prophet ﷺ, said to Mūʿādh رضي الله عنه:

> Whoever testifies with a sincere heart that there is no deity worthy of worship in truth except Allāh alone and that Muḥammad ﷺ is the Messenger of Allāh, then Allāh makes the fire of Hell *harām* for that person.

Mūʿādh رضي الله عنه said, "Shouldn't I let people know? They will be happy to hear that."

The Prophet ﷺ said:

> They will end up becoming complacent and relying on this.

When Mūʿādh رضي الله عنه was on his deathbed, he narrated this ḥadīth out of fear of the sin for concealing knowledge and not preaching the ḥadīth.[39] [Agreed upon]

These aḥādīth prove that having the sincere confession with the declaration of *Īmān*, despite having shortcomings in performing deeds, will one day benefit the individual if they do not associate partners with Allāh.

Abū Dhar رضي الله عنه narrated that the Prophet ﷺ said:

> The servant who states that there is no deity worthy of worship in truth except Allāh and dies upon this, he will go to Paradise.

39 *Saḥīḥ Bukhārī* ḥadīth no.128, *Saḥīḥ Muslim* ḥadīth no.32

Upon hearing this, Abū Dhar 🙼 asked, even if he committed adultery and theft?

The Prophet 🙼 replied:

(Yes), even if he committed adultery and theft.

Abū Dhar 🙼 then asked again, even if he committed adultery and theft?

The Prophet 🙼 once again replied:

Even if he commits adultery and theft, even if Abū Dhar's nose is covered with dust.

Then whenever Abū Dhar 🙼 used to narrate this ḥadīth he would mention, "Even if Abū Dhar's nose is covered in dust."[40]

Doing Major Sins Does Not Rule Out Forgiveness

It is known from the previous chapter that committing a major sin does not mean that one cannot achieve forgiveness, rather every sin is forgiven through repentance.

Sometimes in uncommon circumstances a person's major sin is forgiven without forgiveness, but the servant may not be aware of it. If a person has committed adultery or committed theft and it has been covered up, then Allāh will either forgive him or punish him. If he is punished in this world, then it will mean that he has been punished for his sin, and in the Hereafter he will not be punished for it.

ʿUbādah Bin al-Ṣāmit narrated that the Prophet 🙼 said:

---

40 *Ṣaḥīḥ al-Bukhārī* ḥadīth no.5489, *Ṣaḥīḥ Muslim* ḥadīth no.94

> He who testifies that there is no deity worthy of worship in truth except Allāh, He is the One (and only true deity), He has no partner to Him, and (believes with certainty) that Muḥammad ﷺ is His slave and His Messenger, and also testifies that Īsā ﷺ is Allāh's slave and Messenger, the son of his female slave (Maryam) and (created from) the word of Allāh, which Allāh had sent to Maryam and the soul (created by) Allāh, (in addition he bears witness that) Paradise and Hell are true (and exist) then Allāh will admit such a servant to Paradise, no matter what his deeds are."[41] [Agreed upon]

That is, whether his deeds are good or bad, a great amount or a small amount, in any case, Allāh will admit him to Paradise.

In the narration of Janādah there are additional words to the above mentioned ḥadīth as follows:

> ...he will be able to enter Paradise through any of its doors he wants to.[42] [Reported by al-Bukhārī and the words are from it]

Whichever door you choose to enter into the everlasting Paradise
(Then) all of them are good.

From the previous ḥadīth it is clear that in order to have complete *Īmān*, it is necessary to believe in the previous Prophets and Messengers. Testifying and declaring the *Shahādatayn*[43] is in fact attesting

41 *Saḥīḥ al-Bukhārī* ḥadīth no.3252, *Saḥīḥ Muslim* ḥadīth no.28

42 *Saḥīḥ al-Bukhārī* ḥadīth no.3252

43 [TN] Commonly known as the testimony of faith i.e. declaring that there is no deity worthy of worship in truth except Allah and that Muḥammad ﷺ is His Messenger

to this same command. In addition to this, bearing witness to the other matters mentioned in the ḥadīth will also take a person to Paradise, even if there is fault and negligence in his actions, however this does not prove that evil deeds will not be punished. Since it is also possible that after individuals are punished for their evil deeds, they will then be released from Hell and then admitted to Paradise.

Atonement For Sins

'Amr Bin al-'Āṣ narrated: I came to the service of the Messenger of Allāh and said, "O Messenger of Allāh! Please put your hand out because I want to declare my allegiance to you." When the Prophet extended his hand, I withdrew my hand. The Prophet asked:

> O 'Amr ! What happened to you?

I said, "I want to make a condition (before I declare my allegiance)." The Prophet asked:

> What condition do you want to make?

I said, "The condition is that I want all my previous sins to be forgiven (for my acceptance of Islām)." The Prophet said:

> Do you not know that (accepting) Islām erases past sins and emigration (for the sake of Allāh) also erases this (i.e. previously accumulated sins) and Ḥajj also erases the (sins) that have happened before it.[44] [Reported by Muslim]

From this, it becomes clear that Islām, migration and Ḥajj are the

44 *Saḥīḥ Muslim* ḥadīth no.121

deeds that erase past sins. The implication of the words of the ḥadīth is that a person's sins, whether minor or major, are forgiven by accepting Islām, migrating and performing Ḥajj. With regards to the rights of people, it is possible that Allāh forgives them as well, and He grants Paradise to the oppressed and forgives the oppressor.

There is disbelief before Islām, by testifying with the words of the Shahādatayn and reverting to Islām, the disbelief is removed. Whereas migration and Ḥajj take place after reverting to Islām. Some of the ways for a person to get rid of the sins committed ignorantly whilst being a Muslim are:

If they are in the land of disbelief then they migrate to the land of Islām peacefully. If they do not get the opportunity, then they should try to perform the obligatory Ḥajj if they can afford it. The sign of an accepted Ḥajj and forgiveness of sins is that the condition and life after Ḥajj is better than the previous condition and life in terms of deeds.

Sincerity of Intention

If a person's migration is for the attainment of some worldly purpose, such as a man migrating in order to marry a woman, or a woman migrating with the intention of going there and marrying a man to become a wife, then there is no reward for this migration. Just as in the time of the Prophet ﷺ a man migrated to marry a woman named Umm Qays.[45]

45 *Al-Mu'jam al-Kabīr of al-Ṭabarānī* vol no.9 pg no.103, Ibn Ḥajar declared the *Isnād* as authentic on the conditions of al-Bukhārī and Muslim, *Fatḥul Bārī* vol no.1 pg no.10

Such a person is deprived of reward because deeds are valid with the correct intentions and not with whatever is displayed as apparent.

ʿUmar Bin al-Khaṭṭāb ﷺ narrated that the Messenger of Allāh ﷺ said:

> The reward of deeds depends upon the intentions and every person will get the reward according to what he has intended. Whoever emigrates to Allāh and His Messenger, his emigration will be to Allāh and His Messenger. Whoever emigrates for worldly benefits or for a woman to marry, his emigration was for what he emigrated for.[46] [Agreed upon]

This ḥadīth is one of the great principles and foundations of the religion. All deeds revolve around this ḥadīth. Therefore, the situation of Ḥajj is that if it is performed with the intention of performing the obligatory duty according to the Sharīʿah, then it will be a means of removing sins, and if one performs Ḥajj for the sake of any worldly benefits, then superficially he would have completed his obligation. However, this so called pilgrim will only get what he intended. For example, if a man has a disagreement with his wife and then he goes to Makkah to spend time away, or he goes there in order to earn a living by using Ḥajj as an excuse, or to spend some time outside of his hometown due to the distress and grief that his relatives are causing to him, or he wants to marry someone because he cannot in the place where is he currently residing. In summary, whatever the intention the person had, then they will only obtain that which they intended and they will not get the reward of Ḥajj.

46 *Saḥīḥ al-Bukhārī* ḥadīth no.1, 54, 2392, *Saḥīḥ Muslim* ḥadīth no.1907

Entry Into Paradise and Salvation From Hell, But How?

Mū'ādh ؓ narrated that I asked the Messenger of Allāh ﷺ, "Tell me of an action that will take me to Paradise and save me from Hell." He ﷺ said:

> You have asked me about a very difficult thing, but it is easy for the person on whom Allāh has made it easy. Worship Allāh alone in truth and do not associate anything with Him, establish *Ṣalāh*, pay the (obligatory) *Zakāh*, fast the month of Ramadhān and perform Ḥajj to the House of Allāh.

Then the Prophet ﷺ said:

> Shall I not tell you some more doors of goodness? Fasting is a shield (from the punishment of Hell) and charity erases sin in the same way that water extinguishes fire. An individual who prays at night (is a cause for the removal of sins).

The Prophet ﷺ then added:

> Shall I not tell you about the pillars and the high peak of this matter (religion)?

I said, "Yes." So the Prophet ﷺ said:

> The head of the religion is Islām, its pillar is *Ṣalāh* and its high peak is *Jīhād*.

The Prophet ﷺ then asked:

> Shall I not tell you the basis of all this?

I replied, "Yes! (of course)", the Prophet ﷺ held his tongue and said:

> Restrain this (from useless talk).

I asked, "O Prophet of Allāh ﷺ, will we be taken into account for what we say in terms of talking and discussing?" He ﷺ said:

> O Mū'ādh! May your mother cry over you. Are the people not thrown into the fire upon their faces or noses except because of what their tongues have produced (in terms of evil speech).[47] [Narrated by Aḥmad, al-Tirmidhī and Ibn Mājah]

From this ḥadīth, it is known that good deeds are required to enter Paradise and the doer of these deeds will enter Paradise without going to the fire. Whoever sincerely confesses the two testimonies, but commits negligence in righteous deeds, will be saved in the end, but only after entering Hell. The proofs of which are as follows:

'Ubādah Bin al-Ṣāmit ﷺ narrated that the Prophet ﷺ said:

> Whoever testifies that there is no deity worthy of worship in truth except Allāh and that Muhammad is the Messenger of Allāh, then Allāh has made the fire of Hell *harām* for that person.[48] [Reported by Muslim and al-Tirmidhī]

'Uthmān ﷺ narrated from the Prophet ﷺ that:

> Whoever dies in the state of knowing in truth that there is no deity worthy of being worshipped except Allāh, he will go to Paradise.[49] [Reported by Muslim]

---

47 *Musnad Aḥmad* vol no.5 pg no.331, *Sunan at-Tirmidhī* ḥadīth no.2616, *Sunan Ibn Mājah* ḥadīth no.3973. at-Tirmidhī stated that this ḥadīth is *Hasan Saḥīḥ*

48 *Saḥīḥ Muslim* ḥadīth no.29, *Sunan at-Tirmidhī* ḥadīth no.2638

49 *Saḥīḥ Muslim* ḥadīth no.93

In the narration of ʿUbādah Bin al-Ṣāmit ﵁ the Prophet ﷺ stated dependence on a statement whilst in the narration of ʿUthmān ﵁ he stated that only knowledge of *Tawḥīd* is sufficient. This is because sometimes when an individual is on their deathbed their speech stops working and no words come out of their mouth, but if there is true belief in the testimony of faith in the heart, then there is hope of salvation.

Jābir ﵁ narrated that a man asked, "O Messenger of Allāh ﷺ what are the two things that decide a person's end?" He ﷺ said:

> Whoever dies without associating anything with Allāh will enter Paradise, and whoever dies while associating anything with Allāh will enter the Fire.[50] [Reported by Muslim]

It is stated in this ḥadīth that the entrance to Paradise and Hell depends on either committing *Shirk* or not committing *Shirk*. The rest of the deeds are not mentioned in it because a *Muwaḥḥid* person is never empty of doing righteous deeds since having pure *Tawḥīd* is also a righteous deed, rather it is the highest form of obedience and the most noble of deeds. This is why even if the *Muwaḥḥid* does not have any other good deeds, one day he will get out of Hell and go to Paradise even if this is after hundreds or thousands of years.

In a narration reported by Abū Hurayrah ﵁ he stated that the Prophet ﷺ said:

> Whoever you meet beyond this wall that testifies that there is no deity worthy of being worshipped in truth except Allāh, with certainty in his heart, give him the glad tidings of Para-

50 *Saḥīḥ Muslim* ḥadīth no.93

dise.

(Abū Hurayrah ﷺ met 'Umar ﷺ behind the wall and narrated to him what the Prophet ﷺ said. However 'Umar ﷺ struck Abū Hurayrah ﷺ on the chest making him fall down, so he went back to the Prophet ﷺ in tears. 'Umar ﷺ then proceeded to follow him.)

'Umar ﷺ then stated, (O Messenger of Allāh ﷺ)...I fear that the people will (become complacent and) rely on this glad tiding. Therefore, let the people carry on striving (to do good deeds). The Messenger of Allāh ﷺ said:

> "Yes, let them."[51] [Reported by Muslim]

In the above ḥadīth, the intention of the Prophet ﷺ was to explain that the one who is sincere and a true *Muwaḥḥid* will definitely end up in Paradise, although those who confess true *Tawḥīd* may not enter Paradise initially.

Mū'ādh Bin Jabal ﷺ narrated a ḥadīth in *marfū'* form which includes the following words:

> Testifying to the statement that there is no deity worthy of being worshipped in truth except Allāh alone is the key to Paradise.[52] [Reported by Aḥmad]

It is narrated in a long narration from 'Uthmān ﷺ that Abū Bakr as-Ṣiḍḍīq ﷺ said, "O Messenger of Allāh ﷺ, what is salvation according to this matter (religion)?" He ﷺ said:

---

51 *Saḥīḥ Muslim* ḥadīth no.31

52 *Musnad Ahmad* vol no.5 pg no.242. This *Isnād* is weak however its meaning is correct from other reports

> Whoever accepts from me the words which I offered to my uncle (Abū Ṭālib), and he (my uncle) rejected it, then those words will be the cause of salvation for him.[53] [Reported by Aḥmad]

In this ḥadīth, the word means to testify the statement that there is no deity worthy of being worshipped in truth except Allāh alone. That is, only the one who believes and testifies to this word with sincerity of heart will be given salvation.

One of the virtues of this word is that a person who has reached the level of *Ihsān* in his Islām, his good deeds are multiplied by seven times to ten times, while his sin is written as one sin, up until he passes away and reaches the afterlife. This virtue comes from performing righteous deeds, and whoever does not do righteous deeds is deprived of this advancement, even if he is given salvation at some point.

He who is deprived of the pleasure of obedience (by not doing good deeds except having Tawḥīd)

I am confident that he will certainly be admitted to Paradise

But (initially) he may have to bear the scars and wounds of deprivation (as he may be delayed entry into Paradise due to neglect of good deeds)

Mū'ādh Bin Jabal ﷺ narrated in *marfū'* form that a person who meets Allāh (after their death) in such a state that they do not associate anything with Allāh, performs the five obligatory daily *Ṣalāh* and fasts the month of Ramadhān then they will be forgiven. I said,

53 *Musnad Aḥmad* vol no.1 pg no.6

O Messenger of Allāh ﷺ shall I not give the good news to the people? The Prophet ﷺ said:

> Leave them to do (other righteous) deeds (as well).[54] [Reported by Aḥmad]

In this ḥadīth, forgiveness is specified with the condition that obligatory deeds are performed.

Abū Hurayrah ؓ narrated: I said, "O Messenger of Allāh ﷺ who will be the most deserving and privileged of the intercession of the Prophet ﷺ on the Day of Resurrection?" The Messenger of Allāh ﷺ said:

> I thought that no one would ask me this question before you, because I see that you have a great desire and eagerness to learn the knowledge of ḥadīth. The most deserving person who will have my intercession on the Day of Resurrection will be the one who said sincerely from (the bottom of) his heart that none has the right to be worshipped in truth except Allāh.[55] [Reported by al-Bukhārī]

It is known from this that if a person is a *Muwaḥḥid* in terms of his *Aqīdah* but is negligent with regards to deeds then he will need the intercession for his salvation and whosoever has wide ranging good deeds then he will go to Paradise without reckoning.

Zayd Bin Arqam ؓ narrates in *marfu'* form that:

---

54 *Musnad Aḥmad* vol no.5 pg no.228 and 232. The *Isnād* is authentic on the conditions of al-Bukhārī and Muslim

55 *Saḥīḥ al-Bukhārī* ḥadīth no.99

Whoever sincerely states that there is no deity worthy of being worshipped in truth except Allāh, will go to Paradise.

It was asked what is this type of sincerity? He said:

That this statement prevents him from committing anything that Allāh has made *ḥarām*.[56] [Reported by at-Ṭabarānī in *al-Awsaṭ* with a weak *Isnād*]

Rifāʿah al-Juhanī ☀ narrated that the Prophet ☀ said:

I testify with Allāh that whoever dies by sincerely testifying that there is no deity worthy of being worshipped in truth except Allāh and that I am the Messenger of Allāh, then he stands firm on it, will enter Paradise.[57] [Narrated by Ahmad with an *Isnād* that has no problem in it]

In this ḥadīth, the meaning of standing firm is that he acts in accordance to the statement mentioned above, i.e. the *Kalimah*.

The following words have been narrated from Abū Hurayrah ☀ in *marfūʿ* form:

No worshipper has ever said none has the right to be worshipped in truth except Allāh (the *Kalimah*) sincerely, except that the gates of Paradise are opened for him, until it reaches to the Throne, so long as he avoids the major sins.[58] [Narrated by at-Tirmidhī and he said that this ḥadīth is *ḥasan gharīb*]

Abū Hurayrah also narrates in another ḥadīth with the words:

---

56 *Al-Muʿjam al-Awsaṭ* vol no.2 pg no.52. This *Isnād* is weak
57 *Musnad Aḥmad* vol no.4 pg no.16
58 *Sunan at-Tirmidhī* ḥadīth no.3590

Whoever recites none has the right to be worshipped in truth except Allāh (the *Kalimah*) then these words will surely benefit him one day, even if he has to suffer some punishment.[59] [Reported by al-Bazzār and at-Ṭabarānī]

That is, even if he is punished in Hell, he will eventually be saved.

Abū Saʿīd al-Khudrī 🙵 narrated that Mūsā 🙼 asked Allāh for a special type of *Dhikr* for himself in order to remember Him by. So Allāh said:

O Mūsā, say none has the right to be worshipped in truth except Allāh (the *Kalimah*).

Mūsā 🙼 said:

O my Rabb, all your servants read it.

Allāh said:

If the seven Heavens and seven Earths are put on one side of the scale and the *Kalimah* is put on the other side of the scale then the *Kalimah* will outweigh everything.[60] [Reported by an-Nasāʾī and Ibn Ḥibbān. Al-Ḥakim said that it has a *Ṣaḥīḥ Isnād*]

Similarly, in a ḥadīth narrated from Jābir 🙵 it is mentioned that the statement none has the right to be worshipped in truth except Allāh (the *Kalimah*) has been declared the best *Dhikr*. [Reported by Ibn

---

59 *Musnad al-Bazzār* vol no.15 pg no.22, *Saḥīḥ Ibn Ḥibbān* vol no.7 pg no.272

60 *Sunan an-Nasāʾī* vol no. 6 pg no.208, *Saḥīḥ Ibn Ḥibbān* vol no.14 pg no.102, *Mustadrak al-Ḥākim* vol no.1 pg no.710

Mājah and an-Nasāʾī and Ibn Ḥibbān. Imām Ḥakim said that this ḥadīth has a *Ṣaḥīḥ Isnād*.

Yaʿla Bin Shaddād says that Abū Shaddād Bin Aws said to us in the presence of ʿUbādah Bin Ṣāmit 🙵 and ʿUbādah Bin Ṣāmit 🙵 used to confirm this, that we were with the Messenger of Allāh 🙵 when he said, "Are there any poor (strangers) among you from the People of the Book?" We said, "No." Then the Prophet 🙵 said, "Close the door and raise your hand and say none has the right to be worshipped in truth except Allāh (the *Kalimah*)." So we raised our hands for a while. Then the Prophet 🙵 said, "All complete perfect praise is for Allāh alone. O Allāh! You have sent me with this word none has the right to be worshipped in truth except Allāh (the *Kalimah*) and promised me Paradise over it and you do not break the promise." Then he 🙵 said, "Glad tidings, certainly Allāh has forgiven you."[61] [Reported by Aḥmad with a *ḥasan isnād* and at-Ṭabarānī etc.]

Abū Hurayrah 🙵 narrated in *marfuʿ* form that the Messenger of Allāh 🙵 said, "Renew your faith!" We said, O Messenger of Allāh 🙵, how do we renew our faith? So he 🙵 said, "Recite none has the right to be worshipped in truth except Allāh (the *Kalimah*) frequently."[62] [Reported by Aḥmad and at-Ṭabarānī. The *Isnād* by Aḥmad is *ḥasan*]

ʿUmar 🙵 narrated in *marfuʿ* form that:

I know of a word which, if a person recites it sincerely and then dies on it, then Allāh forbids the fire of Hell for him.

---

61 *Musnad Aḥmad* vol no.4 pg no.124, *al-Muʿjam al-Kabīr of at-Ṭabarānī* vol no.7 pg no.289
62 *Musnad Aḥmad* vol no.2 pg no.309

That word is none has the right to be worshipped in truth except Allāh (the *Kalimah*).[63] [Reported by al-Ḥakim and he said it is *Ṣaḥīḥ* on the conditions of al-Bukhārī and Muslim and he narrated it with a similar wording]

The words of a ḥadīth narrated from Abū Hurayrah ⬥ in *marfu'* form are as follows:

Testify to (*Tawḥīd*) frequently with the words none has the right to be worshipped in truth except Allāh (the *Kalimah*) before anything gets in the way between you and these words." [Reported by Abū Ya'lā with a good and strong *Isnād*]

Meaning, recite these words frequently before death comes to you.

Some scholars have said that a person who recites none has the right to be worshipped in truth except Allāh (the *Kalimah*) seventy thousand times in his lifetime will be forgiven.[64]

Anas ⬥ narrated in *marfū'* form that:

If any servant of Allāh recites none has the right to be worshipped in truth except Allāh (the *Kalimah*) at any time of the day or night, then this word erases all the sins recorded in his book of deeds and all his sins become good deeds.[65] [Reported by Abū Ya'lā]

Meaning that his sins are erased and they are replaced with an equal

---

63 *Mustadrak al-Ḥākim* vol no.1 pg no.134, *Ṣaḥīḥ Ibn Ḥibbān* vol no.1 pg no.343

64 [TN] This saying of some scholars is without any evidence and farfetched, this amount has not been mentioned in any aḥadīth.

65 *Musnad Abī Ya'lā Mūṣilī* vol no.6 pg no.294. This narration is weak.

amount of good deeds.

Ibn 'Umar ﷺ narrated in *marfū'* form that:

> Those who recite none has the right to be worshipped in truth except Allāh (the *Kalimah*) will have no fright or fear in the grave and on the day of resurrection. It is as if I can see the reciters of these words removing the dust from their heads and saying, "All complete praise is for Allāh alone who has removed grief from us."

The words of another narration are as follows:

> Those who recite none has the right to be worshipped in truth except Allāh (the *Kalimah*) will not be frightened at the time of death and in the grave.[66] [However its *Isnād* is very weak. Reported by at-Ṭabarānī]

Ibn 'Umar ﷺ narrated that the Messenger of Allāh ﷺ said:

> Shall I not inform you of the advice which Nūh ﷺ gave to his son?

We said, "Yes (please do so)." So, the Prophet ﷺ said:

> He said to his son, "I advise and instruct you to recite none has the right to be worshipped in truth except Allāh (the *Kalimah*). If this word is placed on one side of the scale and all the Heavens and the Earth are placed on the other side of the scale, then this word will be heavy. If all the Heavens and the Earth take the form of a circle, then this word will break through

66 *Al-Mu'jam al-Awṣaṭ of at-Ṭabarānī* vol no.9 pg no.181. This narration is weak.

them and reach Allāh."[67] [Reported al-Bazzār and the narrators have been validated to be taken as proofs in the Ṣaḥīḥ]

Al-Ḥākim has said that this ḥadīth has a *Ṣaḥīḥ Isnād*.

Imām al-Ḥākim reported a narration as follows:

> I command you to recite none has the right to be worshipped in truth except Allāh (the *Kalimah*). If all the Heavens and the Earth and all things between them are placed on one scale and none has the right to be worshipped in truth except Allāh (the *Kalimah*) is placed on the other, then this *Kalimah* will be heavier than all of them. If all the Heavens and the Earth and all that is in them were a circle and a ring, and you were to put the words none has the right to be worshipped in truth except Allāh (the *Kalimah*) on them, then this word would break them. I command you to recite glory be to Allāh and all complete praise belongs to Him. This is the basis of all things, and everything receives sustenance through it.[68]

The narration which Imām al-Tirmidhī reported from 'Abdullah Bin 'Amr ﵄ in *marfū'* form has the following words:

> As for none has the right to be worshipped in truth except Allāh (the *Kalimah*), there is no barrier to it from Allāh until it reaches Him.[69]

Imām al-Tirmidhī has declared this ḥadīth to be *Gharīb*.

---

67 *Ṣaḥīḥ at-Targhīb and Tarhīb* vol no.2 pg no.104

68 *Mustadrak al-Ḥākim* vol no.1 pg no.112, *Ṣaḥīḥ at-Targhīb and Tarhīb* vol no.2 pg no.105

69 *Sunan at-Tirmidhī* ḥadīth no.3518. This *Isnād* is weak

Ibn 'Umar ☙ narrated that the Messenger of Allāh ☙ said:

> On the Day of Resurrection, Allāh will summon one person from my Ummah in front of all the creatures and open ninety-nine registers before him. Each register will be as far as the eye can see. Then Allāh will say, "Do you deny any of them? Have my scribes wronged you?" He will answer, "O my Rabb! No." Allāh will say, "Do you have any excuse?" He will say: "O my Rabb! No." Allāh will say, "Rather you have a good deed with Us so you will not be wronged today." Then a piece of paper (card) will be taken out in which it will be written, I testify that there is no deity worthy of worship in truth except Allāh and I testify that Muḥammad is His slave and Messenger. Allāh will say, "Go to your weighing area and weigh scales (weight bridge)." He will say, "O my Rabb! What is the status of this piece of paper in front of these registers?" It will be said, "You will not be wronged." Then all those registers will be placed on one pan of the scale and that piece of paper will be placed on the other pan of the scale. All the registers will be light and the piece of paper (with the *Kalimah* written on it) will be heavy because nothing can be heavier than the name of Allāh.[70] [Reported by at-Tirmidhī and it is *Ḥasan*, and Ibn Mājah, Ibn Ḥibbān, al-Bayhaqī and al-Ḥākim who declared it *Ṣaḥīḥ* on the conditions of Muslim]

Definition of *Īmān*

Imām an-Nawawī wrote in his commentary of *Ṣaḥīḥ Muslim* that, linguistically *Īmān* means confirmation, and in the Sharī'ah *Īmān*

---

70 *Sunan at-Tirmidhī* ḥadīth no.2639

means confirmation by the heart and actions done by the limbs.[71]

Imām Ibn Baṭṭal has said that a group of the early scholars and later scholars are of the viewpoint that *Īmān* is a statement of the tongue and actions done by the limbs which increases and decreases.

Therefore, a believer is one who affirms *Īmān* with his heart, confesses it on his tongue and performs actions with his limbs. The *Madhhab* of the *Imāms* from the early scholars is in obvious agreement with the issue that *Īmān* can increase and decrease.

Imām an-Nawawī said:

> (The issue of *Īmān* increasing and decreasing), this is the *madhhab* of the early scholars, Muḥaddīthīn and a group from the Mutakalīmīn... As for the issue of using the word actions/deeds to be part of *Īmān* then the people of truth have an agreed upon consensus on this issue. The evidence for this in the Qur'ān and Sunnah is mentioned countless times.

Abū Hurayrah ﷺ narrated that:

> One day while the Prophet ﷺ was sitting out for the people with his companions, (a man - the Angel) Jibrīl came to him and asked, "What is *Īmān*" Allāh's Messenger ﷺ replied, "*Īmān* is to believe in Allāh, His Angels, (the) meeting with Him, His Messengers, and to believe in Resurrection." Then he further asked, what is Islām? Allāh's Messenger ﷺ replied, "(Islām is) to worship Allāh alone and not associate anyone

---

71 *Sharh Ṣaḥīḥ Muslim of al-Nawawī* vol no.2 pg no.4, *Sunan Abī Dāwūd* ḥadīth no.4300, *Ṣaḥīḥ Ibn Ḥibbān* vol no.1 pg no.461, *Shu'abul Īmān* vol no.1 pg no.264, *Mustadrak al-Ḥākim* vol no.1 pg no.710

with Him in worship, to perform the *Ṣalāh* (prayers), to pay the obligatory *Zakāh* and to observe *Ṣawm* (fasting) during the month of Ramadhān." Then he further asked, what is *Ihsān*? Allāh's Messenger ﷺ replied, "To worship Allāh as if you see Him, and if you cannot achieve this state of devotion then you must consider that He is looking at you."[72] [Reported by Muslim]

Qaḍī 'Iyād stated that:

> In the above mentioned ḥadīth (ḥadīth of Jibrīl) there is a description and explanation of the benefits of all the outward and inward acts of worship. Whether they are the beliefs of *Īmān*, deeds done by the limbs and concealed sincerity or protection from the calamities of deeds, everything is mentioned within it. All the sciences of Sharī'ah return to it and branch from it. I have compiled the book *Al-Maqāṣid ul-Hisān Fīmā Yalzim ul-Insān* on the basis of the ḥadīth of Jibrīl, because whether it is obligatory, *Sunan*, encouragements, precautions or prohibitions, then all of them fall under one of the answers to the three questions (about Islām, *Īmān* and *Ihsān*) mentioned in the ḥadīth.[73]

The *madhhab* of the researchers of Islām and the majority of scholars from the early and later generations is that when a person transcends doubt and becomes a believer in Islām with conviction and readiness then he becomes a *Muwaḥḥid* believer. Now learning the arguments of the *Mutakalīmīn* concerning knowledge of Allāh is not obligatory because the

---

72 *Ṣaḥīḥ al-Bukhārī* ḥadīth no.50, *Ṣaḥīḥ Muslim* ḥadīth no.9

73 *Sharḥ Ṣaḥīḥ Muslim of al-Nawawī* vol no.1 pg no.158

Prophet ﷺ mentioned that with regards to *Īmān*, it is adequate to only confirm it and did not make it a condition to acquire knowledge of it with evidence. There are so many aḥādīth reported in the two *Ṣaḥīḥs* to prove this that when bringing them all together it becomes so frequent to the level of being definitive and certain knowledge.[74]

The One Who Abandons the Pillars of Islām Is a Disbeliever and His Blood and Wealth Are *Halal*

The Bedouins who are present in large numbers on the Earth and are content to recite only the utterances of the *Kalimah* and testimony of *Īmān* and abandon the pillars of Islām, rather they abandon all the obligations of Islām. They also abandon all of the statements and deeds which are obligatory on them so they have nothing but the recitation of the *Kalimah*. Then for certain they are disbelievers and their blood and wealth are lawful because blood and wealth are only safe when a person is dutiful to the pillars of Islām.

The ruling regarding such people is that they should be guided to the right path through preaching and admonition and if they do not follow the straight path and persist upon their disbelief then it is allowed to fight against them[75] because they are under the ruling of the people of ignorance.

74 *Sharḥ Ṣaḥīḥ Muslim of Nawawī* vol no.1 pg no.211
75 [TN] Under the command of the Muslim state ruler just as Abū Bakr ؓ launched military campaigns against the rebellious Arab tribes who refused to give the obligatory *Zakāh*

Who Is Responsible for Fighting the Blasphemous Disbelievers?

The truth is that according to the *āyāt* and aḥādīth of the Prophet ﷺ, it is obligatory on every believer to fight such people (in Darul Ḥarb) without the observance of the *Imām* of the time. [Mentioned by ash-Shawkānī][76]

Ruling on the Individual Who Commits a Major Sin and Dies Without Repentance

Imām an-Nawawī said,

> The *madhhab* of Ahlus Sunnah Wal Jamā'ah, on which the people of the truth from the early and later scholars are agreed upon, is that whoever dies as a *Muwaḥḥid* will definitely go to Paradise in any case. Therefore if they are safe from sins, such as a small child who has not reached the age of puberty, the insane, or if they have committed a sin then truly repented from it and is safe from sins such as *Shirk* etc., while they have not committed any sin after repentance, or they are such a person of great ability that they have not (committed a major) sin at all, then all these kinds of people will enter Paradise and will never go to Hell. Yes, they will arrive at Hell however there is also a difference of opinion on this view. The correct position

76 [TN] *Al-Fathur Rabbānī Min Fatāwā Al-Imām Ash-Shawkānī* pg no.4494 – 4495. This is referring to those disbelievers who are in Darul Ḥarb and not the disbelievers in those countries where Muslims are living peacefully with, such as Britain. Whichever area has become Darul Ḥarb then the general Muslims will not wait for someone to become a leader in order to fight and defend themselves against the disbelievers.

is that it means crossing the bridge that will be placed over Hell.

Whoever commits a major sin and dies without repenting then they are under the will of Allāh, that is whether He forgives them and takes them to Paradise makes them like the first kind of people to enter Paradise or if He wills then He can punish them with the amount of penalty that is given according to the sin based on how much He intends, and then admit them to Paradise. However, whosoever dies upon *Tawḥīd* no matter what their deeds and sins may be, they will not stay in Hell forever, in contrast just as a person who dies on disbelief, even if the disbeliever has done all other good deeds, they will never go to Paradise.

I seek refuge in Allāh from this and from all other evils.

This is a brief and comprehensive discussion based on the *madhhab* of the people of truth for the above issue. The arguments of the Qur'ān and Sunnah on this ruling and the consensus of the esteemed people of the Ummah are obvious. There are so many texts on it, through which certainty and definite knowledge is obtained for this issue. When this ruling has been proven and established, then all the aḥādīth that have been narrated on this issue, etc., will be applied to it in this way. When a ḥadīth appears to be contradictory to this ruling then it is obligatory on us to interpret it, so that the apparent contradictions between the Sharīʿah texts are eliminated and they are reconciled therefore having harmony among them."[77]

77 *Sharḥ Ṣaḥīḥ Muslim of Nawawī* vol no.1 pg no.217

The *Muwaḥḥid* Will Certainly Be in Paradise

There is a long ḥadīth narrated from Abū Hurayrah 🙵 which mentions the battle of Tabūk. In it the Prophet 🙵 said:

> I testify that none has the right to be worshipped in truth except Allāh and that certainly I am the Messenger of Allāh. No one who meets Allāh (believing) in them and not doubting them will not be prevented from (entering) Paradise.

This means that they will enter Paradise after being punished and atoning for their sins.

Qaḍī 'Iyād said:

> It is the *madhhab* of the righteous early scholars, Ahlul ḥadīth, jurists and the Mutakalīmīn Ashā'irah from Ahlus Sunnah that the sinful people are under the will of Allāh. Whosoever dies in the state of *Īmān* and testifies sincerely to the *Shahadatayn* will go to Paradise, provided that they have either repented for their sins or are completely free from sins. It will be possible for them to enter Paradise and be saved from (having to enter) Hell (first) only through the mercy of Allāh.

> If he is one of those people whose good and bad deeds are mixed and he has neglected his obligatory duties and committed *harām*, then he is under the will of Allāh. It cannot be said with certainty that Hell is forbidden for them, nor can it be said with certainty that they deserve to enter Paradise with the first ones who will enter it (i.e. without reckoning). However, what can be said with certainty in their favour is that in the end they will enter Paradise but before that they are at risk of

being under the will of Allāh. Either Allāh can decide to punish them for their sin or He can decide to forgive them out of His bounty.

It is a compulsory and necessary thing for a *Muwaḥḥid* to enter Paradise, either they will be forgiven immediately and quickly then enter Paradise or they will be delayed entry into Paradise and only enter it after being punished for some time. The meaning of the phrases that Hell is *harām* on them means that it is *harām* on them to stay in Hell forever, or that the matter of prohibition is specific to the person whose last words are the *Kalimah* and *Shahadatayn*. This applies even though they may have previously done a mixture of good and bad deeds. However, the reciting of the *Kalimah* now will become a cause of divine mercy and salvation for them from Hell. In contrast those people whose last word is not the *Kalimah* will have the opposite outcome to this. This is the meaning of the above ḥadīth narrated by 'Ubādah ﵁.

Finally the part in which it is mentioned that a person can enter Jannah from any of its doors they wish to, then this is specific for that person who the Prophet ﷺ mentioned and attached the reality of *Īmān* and *Tawḥīd* to the *Shahādatayn*. For example, a person who is rewarded so much that it outweighs their sins and this becomes a means for them to be given mercy, forgiveness and entry with the first entrants of Paradise. [End quote of Qaḍī 'Iyād's words.]

Imām an-Nawawī said that this is a wonderful and excellent explanation.[78]

The Importance and Virtue of Perseverance in Having *Īmān* in Allāh

It is narrated on the authority of Abū Dhar ﵁: I said, "O Messenger of Allāh ﷺ, which deed is the best?" The Prophet ﷺ said:

> Having *Īmān* in Allāh...[79] [Reported by Muslim]

This ḥadīth makes it clear that action applies to *Īmān*. It means, and Allāh knows best, that it is the *Īmān* that brings someone into the religion of Islam, i.e. to affirm with the heart and to recite the *Kalimah* and *Shahādatayn* with the tongue. Therefore, affirmation is the deed of the heart and speech is the deed of the tongue.

Sufyān ath-Thaqafī ﵁ asked the Prophet ﷺ, "O Messenger of Allāh, tell me something about Islām that I will not need to ask anyone about after you." So he ﷺ said:

> Say, I believe in Allāh, then adhere firmly to that.

Qaḍī 'Iyād said:

> This ḥadīth is from the *Jawami'ul Kalim* and is in accordance with Allāh's statement:
>
> إِنَّ الَّذِينَ قَالُوا رَبُّنَا اللَّهُ ثُمَّ اسْتَقَامُوا ﴿٣٠﴾
>
> **{Surely those who say, "Our Rabb is Allāh," and then**

78 *Sharḥ Ṣaḥīḥ Muslim by al-Nawawī* vol no.1 pg no.220
79 *Ṣaḥīḥ Muslim* ḥadīth no.84

remain steadfast...} [Sūrah Fuṣṣilat: 30]

Meaning to know Allāh is One (without any partners or associates), then to have *Īmān* in Him, then to persevere on this *Tawḥīd* and *Īmān*. Additionally, to not abandon *Tawḥīd* or give up on *Īmān*, rather adhere to obedience until death comes. These are the meanings of this ḥadīth narrated by the companions .

The manifestation of grace descends only on those who persevere
You will not see the manifestation revolving around the mountain

Ibn 'Abbās said: Throughout the Qur'ān, the toughest *āyah* which was revealed upon the Prophet was:

$$\text{فَٱسْتَقِمْ كَمَآ أُمِرْتَ} ﴿١١٢﴾$$

{So be steadfast as you are commanded...} [Sūrah Hūd: 112]

That is why the Companions said to the Prophet that you have grown old very quickly. So he said, "Sūrah Hūd and other similar *Sūrahs* have made me old."[80]

Perseverance Is the Means Towards Achieving Perfection

Qūshayrī has said in his short treatise that:

The perfection of all matters is achieved with this same degree of perseverance. The attainment of virtues and the system

---

80 *Sharḥ an-Nawawī* vol no.2 pg no.9

surrounding it is associated with this perseverance. A person who is not going to persevere in any of their situations, then their efforts are wasted and are in vain. No one except the best people have the strength to persevere because in order to do this the individual has to give up the prevailing strong habits and say goodbye to the customs and traditions. Along with strictly standing before Allāh upon the truth." That is why the Prophet ﷺ said, "Adhere to righteousness even though you will not be able to do all acts of virtue."[81]

Wāsitī said, "This perseverance is the quality by which all virtues are perfected and without this quality all virtues are lost."[82]

Modesty Is Part of *Īmān*

Abū Hurayrah ﷺ narrated that the Prophet ﷺ said:

> Modesty is a branch of *Īmān*.[83] [Reported by Muslim]

The people of knowledge have said that the reason why modesty is considered a branch of *Īmān* is because sometimes it is gained through imitating others and therefore it requires an effort to learn this trait like all other good deeds and sometimes this modesty is natural. However, its use in the Sharī'ah depends on making an effort to learn this trait with the correct intention, that is why it is called (a part of) *Īmān*, because it stimulates good deeds and prevents one

81 *Sunan Ibn Mājah* ḥadīth no.278, *Ṣaḥīḥ at-Targhīb Wat-Tarhīb* vol no.1 pg no.48
82 *Sharḥ an-Nawawī* vol no.2 pg no.9
83 *Ṣaḥīḥ Muslim* ḥadīth no.35

from committing sins and wrongdoings.

Abū Qatādah narrated that the Prophet ﷺ said:

> Modesty does not bring anything but goodness.[84] (Reported by Muslim)

A Problem Related to Modesty and Its Answer

If someone asks: How can modesty be good since sometimes it can prevent someone from facing the truth and accepting it, and can obstruct them to give up the duty of enjoining good and forbidding evil?

So Ibn Ṣalāh and a group of *Imāms* answered this by stating that the condition of modesty is symbolic for the problems cited in the above situation. Whilst in reality modesty is the only thing which can prevent immoral and disgraceful actions as well as prohibit the violation of guardianship and rights.[85]

I say, just as no believer and person with *Īmān* is rude or shameless, equally most people who are rude or shameless do not have *Īmān* and are not believers. You may have seen the disobedient and immoral people not caring about having a good reputation, integrity and any shame. This is why they do not remain steadfast on the deeds of *Īmān*. They always commit harmful and destructive deeds and they never pay attention to the deeds of salvation. They are not ashamed of Allāh, nor of the Messenger of Allāh ﷺ, nor of the pious servants of Allāh. Their *Īmān* is very weak and feeble.

84 *Ṣaḥīḥ Muslim* ḥadīth no.37
85 *Sharḥ an-Nawawī* vol no.2 pg no.5 and 6

Some More Components Of *Īmān*

Being good to neighbours and hospitable to guests is included as being part of *Īmān*. This has been emphasized a lot in the aḥādīth. Abū Shūrayh ﷺ narrated that the Prophet ﷺ said:

> Whoever believes in Allāh and the Last Day, let him treat his neighbour well; whoever believes in Allāh and the Last Day, let him honour his guest; whoever believes in Allāh and the Last Day, let him speak good or else remain silent.[86] [Reported by Muslim]

This also includes discouraging the deniers of *Īmān* with one's hand, tongue or at the very least knowing that it is evil in one's heart. This matter has been narrated from Abū Saʿīd al-Khuḍrī ﷺ in a *marfūʿ ḥadīth*[87]. Removing evil with the hand is the duty of the *Imāms*, rulers and people of *Islām*. Removing evil, changing it and eradicating it with the tongue is the duty of the scholars of the hereafter. Knowing that it is evil in the heart is the duty of the general Muslims and this is the weakest level of *Īmān*.

The Remaining Ritual of *Adhān* of Nowadays Is Not at the Same Lofty Spirit as the *Adhān* of Bilāl ﷺ

It is written in *As-Sirājul Wahhāj* that:

> It seems that *Īmān* has been lost for a long time. It is as if people have taken it for granted and thought of it as an abolished act of the Sharīʿah. Now there is nothing left but a few rituals.

86 *Ṣaḥīḥ Muslim* ḥadīth no.48
87 *Ṣaḥīḥ Muslim* ḥadīth no.49

This is a great issue with which the religion of *Islām* becomes straight and under control. When evil increases in it, then a common punishment comes that inflicts all the good and the bad people. When they do not restrain the hand of the oppressor then it is imminent that Allāh is about to punish them all, as He said:

فَلْيَحْذَرِ الَّذِينَ يُخَالِفُونَ عَنْ أَمْرِهِ أَن تُصِيبَهُمْ فِتْنَةٌ أَوْ يُصِيبَهُمْ عَذَابٌ أَلِيمٌ ﴿٦٣﴾

{So let those who disobey his orders beware, for an affliction may befall them, or a painful torment may overtake them.} [Sūrah an-Nūr: 63]

The seeker of the Hereafter and the one who wants to please Allāh should pay a lot of attention to this because its benefit is very great, provided that his intention is pure and he does not fear the evil at all. This is because Allāh stated:

وَلَيَنصُرَنَّ اللَّهُ مَن يَنصُرُهُ ﴿٤٠﴾

{And Allah will surely support those who support Him (i.e., His cause).} [Sūrah al-Ḥajj: 40]

Allāh also said, "Do the people think that they will be left to say, 'We believe' and they will not be tried?"[88]

Commanding The Good and Forbidding the Evil Are Pillars of the Religion

All Muslims agree that it is obligatory to enjoin what is good and

88 *As-Sirājul Wahhāj* vol no.1 pg no.172, 173

forbid what is evil. These are two great pillars of the religion and are firmly necessary on every Muslim.

Ibn Masʿūd ☙ narrated that the Prophet ☙ said:

> Whoever strives against them with his hand is a believer; whoever strives against them with his tongue is a believer; whoever strives against them with his heart is a believer. Beyond that there is not even a mustard-seed's worth of *Īmān*.[89] [Reported by Muslim in a long ḥadīth]

In this ḥadīth, *Īmān* is denied to the one who does not perform the duty of enjoining the good and forbidding the evil. To the extent that *Īmān* has not been established for him as much as a grain of a mustard-seed. Whereas the one who has *Īmān* equal to the grain of a mustard-seed will eventually gain salvation one day. So whoever does not even have that much *Īmān*, what hope can he have for salvation?

Allāh knows that in this day and age we do not have the power to fully change and eradicate evil with our hands. However, we do not neglect whatever we would have to do that comes from our hearts and tongues, and I cannot accomplish anything except with the power of Allāh.

The Love for ʿAlī ☙ and the Anṣār ☙ Is a Part of *Īmān*

The love for ʿAlī ☙ is also included as being part of one of the levels of *Īmān*. Zirr Bin Ḥubaysh ☙ narrated that ʿAlī ☙ said: By the One Who split the seed and created the soul, the [unlettered] Prophet ☙ affirmed to me:

---

89 *Ṣaḥīḥ Muslim* ḥadīth no.50

No one loves me except a believer and no one hates me except a hypocrite.[90] [Reported by Muslim]

The love for the Anṣār is also a part of *Īmān*. 'Adī Bin Thābit narrated that the Messenger of Allāh said:

No one loves them but a believer, and no one hates them but a hypocrite.[91] [Reported by Muslim]

The Praise of *Īmān* for the People of Yemen and Ḥijāz

The Prophet said:

(True) *Īmān* is among the Yemenis, and (true) wisdom is that of the Yemenis.[92] [Reported by Muslim]

In another narration of *Ṣaḥīḥ Muslim* it is stated that:

(True) understanding is that of the Yemenis.[93] [Reported by Muslim]

Some Qur'ānic *āyāt* have also been revealed in favour of the people of Yemen which indicate and evidence their completeness of *Īmān* as well as their virtue of having (true) wisdom and (true) understanding (of the religion). This (true) wisdom refers to the knowledge and science of ḥadīth.

Additionally, the words of the ḥadīth narrated from Jābir mention the following:

---

90 *Ṣaḥīḥ Muslim* ḥadīth no.78
91 *Ṣaḥīḥ Muslim* ḥadīth no.75
92 *Ṣaḥīḥ Muslim* ḥadīth no.52
93 *Ṣaḥīḥ Muslim* ḥadīth no.52

Īmān is among the people of the Ḥijāz.[94] [Reported by Muslim]

These two aḥadīth prove that *Īmān* is in Yemen and Ḥijāz.

Good Deeds Are Useless Without *Īmān*

'Ā'ishah 🙵 narrates: I asked: "O Messenger of Allāh 🙵, during the pre-Islamic period of ignorance, Ibn Jud'ān used to uphold the ties of kinship and feed the poor. Will that benefit him at all? He 🙵 said:

(No) it will not benefit him, because he did not say (even for) one day: Rabb forgive me my sins on the Day of Judgment.[95] [Reported by Muslim]

This shows that a good deed does not benefit a person who does not have *Īmān* because the one who believes in resurrection after death is a believer and the one who does not confirm it is a disbeliever.

Abū Hurayrah 🙵 narrated that the Messenger of Allāh 🙵 said:

You will not enter Paradise until you (truly) believe.[96] [Reported by Muslim]

Meaning that, it is not possible to enter Paradise without having *Īmān*.

Similarly, Abū Hurayrah 🙵 narrated that the Messenger of Allāh 🙵 said that:

---

94 *Ṣaḥīḥ Muslim* ḥadīth no.53
95 *Ṣaḥīḥ Muslim* ḥadīth no.214
96 *Ṣaḥīḥ Muslim* ḥadīth no.54

No adulterer is a believer at the time he is committing adultery; no thief is a believer at the time he is stealing; no drinker of wine is a believer at the time he is drinking it.[97] [Reported by Muslim]

Abū Hurayrah ☘ also narrated that the Messenger of Allāh ☘ said:

(Having *waswasah* (whispers, bad thoughts) and knowing that they are wrong indicates) that is clear *Īmān*.[98] [Reported by Muslim]

This means that when a person considers *waswasah* to be great and considers it bad then this is the proof of him having *Īmān*. If he did not have *Īmān* then why would he consider these *waswasah* as being something great and bad? When a person makes this type of consideration then it is a sign of his *Īmān*.

Anas Bin Mālik ☘ narrated that the Messenger of Allāh ☘ said:

Allāh does not treat the believer unjustly with regard to his good deeds. He blesses him because of them in this world and He will reward him for them in the Hereafter. As for the disbeliever, he is fed because of the good deeds that he does for the sake of Allāh in this world, then when he passes on into the Hereafter, he will have no good deeds left for which to be rewarded.[99] [Reported by Muslim]

Allāh says:

---

97 *Ṣaḥīḥ Muslim* ḥadīth no.57
98 *Ṣaḥīḥ Muslim* ḥadīth no.132 and no.133
99 *Ṣaḥīḥ Muslim* ḥadīth no.2808

قُلْ تَمَتَّعْ بِكُفْرِكَ قَلِيلًا إِنَّكَ مِنْ أَصْحَابِ النَّارِ ۞

{Say, [O Prophet,] Enjoy your disbelief (and take advantage of your ingratitude) for a little while! You will certainly be one of the inmates of the Fire.} [Sūrah az-Zumar: 8]

Abū Hurayrah ⬭ narrated in *marfūʿ* form that:

Allah has excused and forgiven for my Ummah whatever occurs in themselves (crosses their mind), so long as they do not speak of it - or act upon it.[100] [Reported by Muslim]

Abū Hurayrah ⬭ narrated that the Messenger of Allāh ⬭ said:

Islām began as something strange and will revert to being something strange, so glad tidings to the stranger.[101] [Reported by Muslim]

The meaning and example of this ḥadīth can be seen in the present age to a great extent, but at the same time it has glad tidings for the strange like us. This is provided that we are patient and steadfast in our *Īmān* and *Islām* and do not deviate from them because of the seduction, intimidation and greed of the enemies of Islam. However even this situation has become strange (as there are not many people who are patient and steadfast like this). Allāh knows and you do not know.

Note: The reason why we have mentioned the virtues and benefits of the *Kalimah* here along with the topics of *Īmān* is to demon-

---

100 *Ṣaḥīḥ Muslim* ḥadīth no.127
101 *Ṣaḥīḥ Muslim* ḥadīth no.145

strate that the correctness of the true *Īmān* is connected with the confirmation and sincerity of this *Kalimah* from the bottom of the heart.

When the virtue and benefit of it is known, a zeal and enthusiasm to receive this blessing arises from the heart. A wise person knows very well that when this praiseworthy result is achieved by merely uttering the words of the *Shahādatayn* with a sincere heart, so why wouldn't the individual also attain higher ranks by performing good deeds and following the rules of *Īmān*? The mere attainment of salvation is through having a low degree of *Īmān* and the highest degree of *Īmān* is that an individual attains great success.

The Privileged Ones Who Will Benefit From Intercession

Anas 🌸 narrated a long ḥadīth in *marfūʿ* form about intercession that the Messenger of Allāh 🌸 said:

> I will ask Allāh for permission and every single time (I am given permission) I will intercede and a limit will be set for me (for the people I am going to intercede for). Then I will ask for permission, and then another limit will be set. I will ask for permission to intercede for the third time, then another limit will be set and I will take them out of Hell and admit them to Paradise, until only those who have been detained and forbidden by the Qur'ān (i.e. those who are bound to abide therein forever) will remain in Hell.[102] [Agreed upon]

Staying in Hell forever will be the destiny of the person who is a polytheist or a disbeliever, even if the person is in the guise of a Muslim

---

102 *Ṣaḥīḥ al-Bukhārī* ḥadīth no.7002, *Ṣaḥīḥ Muslim* ḥadīth no.193

and the same rule applies to a hypocrite.

In another narration it is mentioned:

> Whoever has *Īmān* in his heart equal to a grain of barley, I will take him out of Hell. Then I will do the same for he who has *Īmān* in his heart equal to a mustard seed. Then, for the third time, I will take out the person who has *Īmān* in his heart equal to a speck or atom. Then I will say for the fourth time, O Rabb, allow me to intercede for those who recited the *Kalimah* i.e. that there is no deity worthy of being worshipped in truth except Allāh. So Allāh will say: That is not for you, but by My Might, Majesty, Greatness and Power, I shall bring forth whoever said the *Kalimah* i.e. that there is no deity worthy of being worshipped in truth except Allāh."[103]

All complete praise is for Allāh, that is whether we praise Him or we don't, He is still worthy of all praise.

From this it becomes clear that first there would be intercession for the sinners who were not polytheists. Then of those who merely uttered the *Kalimah* and did not associate partners with Allāh, even if they have committed sins in all parts of the world. Our Prophet ﷺ will intercede for us, but only after receiving permission from Allāh and there will also be a limit to this intercession. It will be said that intercession is only allowed for those who did not perform the *Ṣalāh* in congregation or had deficiencies in their *Ṣalāh*. Then the second time it will be said that intercession is allowed for such and such sinners like those who were drunkards or adulterers. In the same way, intercession will be allowed for the third time for another kind of

103 *Ṣaḥīḥ al-Bukhārī ḥadīth* no.7072, *Saḥīḥ Muslim* ḥadīth no.193

people and these will be the limitations set from Allāh.

However, anyone who committed any act of polytheism or disbelief and died without repentance, then they will not be interceded for at all, because they will be restricted from entering Paradise with the Qurʾānic text. Such as the grave worshipers, saint worshippers, hypocrites and other such people. Then in the last intercession, Allāh Himself will save the sincere *Muwaḥḥids* from Hell who did not have any good deeds except sins. After that there will be no one left in Hell except the polytheists and disbelievers.

It Is An Individual Obligation on Every Human Being To Avoid *Shirk*

Shirk (Polytheism) is something that every human being has a duty to avoid. This *shirk* is hidden a lot and it has seventy gates, just as there are seventy two gates of *bidʿah*. Whoever wants to seek salvation and success, they should make a great effort to find out about the gates of *Shirk* and *bidʿah* which is at the level of disbelief because if the individual has worshipped and obeyed Allāh as much as every single person in the world but ends up committing any hidden type of *Shirk* and disbelief, whether that be in their *ʿaqīdah* or in their deeds, then they will certainly not be entitled to the intercession and any form of salvation.

On the other hand, if they have not done any good deeds or have committed sins as much as every single person in the world, but they have saved themselves from committing *shirk*, then one day they will surely get out of Hell and will be forgiven.

In this regard, the treatises of *Taqwīyatul Īmān* and *Duʿāul Īmān* are very useful and comprehensive in explaining this subject with further detail.

Those Who Will Leave Hell

Abū Saʿīd al-Khuḍrī 🕸 narrated in a long ḥadīth with *marfūʿ* form that:

> In the second intercession, Allāh will say to the believers: 'Go back, and whomever you find with a dīnar's weight of goodness in his heart, bring him out'. They will bring out many people, then they will say: 'Our Rabb, we have not left therein any of those whom You commanded us to bring out.'
>
> Then He will say: 'Go back, and whomever you find with half a dīnar's weight of goodness in his heart, bring him out.' They will bring out many people, then they will say: 'Our Rabb, we have not left therein any of those whom You commanded us to bring out.'
>
> Then He will say, 'Go back, and whomever you find with a speck of goodness in his heart, bring him out.' They will bring out many people, then they will say: 'Our Rabb, we have not left any goodness therein.'
>
> Allāh will say: 'The angels have interceded, and the righteous believers have interceded, the Prophets 🕸 have interceded, and there is no one left (to intercede) but the Most Merciful of those who show mercy.' Then He will take a handful from Hell and will bring out people who never did any good and who will have turned into charcoal. He will throw them into

> a river on the outskirts of Paradise that is called the River of Life and they will emerge like seeds from that which is carried by a flood. They will emerge like pearls with jewels around their necks, and the people of Paradise will recognize them. These are the ones ransomed by Allāh, whom Allāh admitted to Paradise with no good deed that they did or sent on ahead.
>
> Then He will say: 'Enter Paradise and whatever you see is yours.' They will say 'Our Rabb, You have given us what You have never given to anyone else in all the worlds.' He will say: 'You will have in Paradise that which you have seen and something better than that with Me.'"[104] [Agreed Upon]

Another narration that has been narrated from Abū Saʿīd Al-Khuḍrī ﷺ includes the following words:

> Allāh will admit the people of Paradise to Paradise and He will admit whomever He wills by His mercy. And He will admit the people of the Fire to the Fire. Then He will say: 'Look, and whomever you find with a mustard-seed's weight of *Īmān* in his heart, bring him out.' They will bring out people who have been burned, like charcoal, then they will be thrown into the River of Life - or Rain from which they will emerge like seeds sprouting at the banks of the flood. Do you not see how they emerge yellow and curved?[105] [Agreed upon]

Ạnas ﷺ narrated in *marfūʿ* form that:

> Some people will be scorched by Hell (Fire) as a punishment

104 *Ṣaḥīḥ al-Bukhārī* ḥadīth no.7001, *Saḥīḥ Muslim* ḥadīth no.183
105 *Ṣaḥīḥ al-Bukhārī* ḥadīth no.22, *Saḥīḥ Muslim* ḥadīth no.184

> for sins they have committed, and then Allah will admit them into Paradise by the grant of His Mercy. These people will be called Jahannamīyūn (the people of Hell).[106] [Reported by al-Bukhārī]

This proves that some sinful *Muwaḥḥids* will also go to Hell, although eventually they will get out of it due to the blessing of *Tawḥīd*, but it is somewhat difficult to be a *Muwaḥḥid*.

Those Who Will Be Worthy and Entitled to the Intercession of the Messenger ﷺ

Anas narrated that the Messenger of Allāh ﷺ said:

> My intercession will be for the people of my Ummah who committed major sins.[107] [Reported by the authors of the famous books of *Sunan*]

ʿAwf Bin Mālik narrated that the Prophet ﷺ said:

> Someone came to me from my Lord to give me the choice between half of my Ummah being admitted into Paradise or intercession. So I chose the intercession and it is for whoever dies and he did not associate anything with Allāh.[108] [Reported by at-Tirmidhī and Ibn Mājah]

---

106 *Ṣaḥīḥ al-Bukhārī* ḥadīth no.7450

107 *Sunan Abī Dāwūd* ḥadīth no.4739, *Sunan at-Tirmidhī* ḥadīth no.2435, *Sunan Ibn Mājah* ḥadīth no.4310, *Ṣaḥīḥ at-Targhīb Wat-Tarhīb* vol no.3 pg no.241

108 *Sunan at-Tirmidhī* ḥadīth no.2441, *Sunan Ibn Mājah* ḥadīth no.4311, *Musnad Aḥmad* vol no.3 pg no.165

Therefore, grave worshipers, saint worshippers and others like them should not expect intercession, because this intercession will be exclusive to the *Muwaḥḥids* only.

Anas narrated that the Messenger of Allāh said:

> Allāh has promised me that He will admit 400,000 people of my Ummah into Paradise.

Abu Bakr said, "Mention more (than this)". The Prophet said:

> Two more filled up handfuls (more).

Abū Bakr then said, "And (again) mention more (than this)". The Prophet said:

> And more amount of people equivalent to these (two handfuls).[109]

[Ḥadīth reported in *Sharḥ as-Sunnah*]

The above ḥadīth shows that the filled-up handful amounts of people that will be taken out of the fire mean Allāh's handful[110]. And all complete praise is due to Allāh.

---

109 *Sharḥ as-Sunnah* vol no.7 pg no.444

110 [TN] The attributes of Allāh are to be understood in a manner that befits His majesty without likening them to anything. The meaning of how this will occur is inconceivable in the mind and should be left without unnecessarily questioning it, just as the companions and Awlīyā of Allāh did so in the past.

Those Who Will Go to Paradise Without Reckoning

Ibn 'Abbās ﷺ narrated in *marfū'* form that the Messenger of Allāh ﷺ said:

> Seventy thousand people of my Ummah will enter Paradise without reckoning. They are the ones who did not perform *Ruqyah* nor ask others to do so, and did not follow omens, and relied upon their Rabb (instead of resorting to other means).[111] [Agreed upon]

The words of the second narration are:

> They are the ones who did not use cauterization or ask others to perform *Ruqyah* for them, and relied upon their Rabb (instead of resorting to other means).

'Ukāshah stood up and said, 'Pray to Allah to make me one of them.'

He ﷺ said:

> You will be one of them.

Another man stood up and said, 'O Prophet of Allāh ﷺ, pray to Allah to make me one of them.' He ﷺ said:

> 'Ukāshah has surpassed you to it.[112] [Agreed upon]

The *Muwaḥḥid* Does Not Rely Upon Anyone Except Allāh

Complete *Īmān* is an expression of *Tawḥīd*. When a person's

111 *Ṣaḥīḥ al-Bukhārī* ḥadīth no.6107, *Ṣaḥīḥ Muslim* ḥadīth no.220
112 *Ṣaḥīḥ al-Bukhārī* ḥadīth no.6107, *Ṣaḥīḥ Muslim* ḥadīth no.218

Tawḥīd is complete he does not rely on anyone at all, no matter who the others are, except Allāh. By doing so, he does not have any expectations or hope in anyone and neither does he fear them. Rather, the ḥadīth narrated by Ibn 'Abbās ﷺ from the Messenger of Allāh ﷺ is before his eyes at every moment, in which Ibn 'Abbās ﷺ said that, 'I was riding behind the Messenger of Allāh ﷺ and he ﷺ said to me':

> O boy! I will teach you a statement: Be mindful of Allāh (and his commands) and He will protect you. Be mindful of Allah (and his commands) and you will find Him before you. When you ask, ask Allah, and when you seek aid, seek Allah's aid. Know that if the entire creation were to gather together to do something to benefit you – you would never get any benefit except what Allah has ordained for you. And if they were to gather to do something to harm you – you would never be harmed except what Allah has ordained for you. The pens are lifted (from writing) and the pages are dried."[113] [Reported by Aḥmad and At-Tirmidhī]

قُل لَّن يُصِيبَنَا إِلَّا مَا كَتَبَ اللَّهُ لَنَا ﴿٥١﴾

> **{Say, 'Nothing will ever befall us except what Allah has destined for us'}** [Sūrah at-Tawbah: 51]

This ḥadīth refers to being satisfied with the destiny ordained by Allāh and His decision. Additionally, this ḥadīth has instructed us to adopt pure *Tawḥīd*.

Mū'ādh ﷺ said: The Messenger of Allāh ﷺ bequeathed to me ten words, one of which is:

---

113 *Musnad Aḥmad* vol no.1 pg no.293, *Sunan at-Tirmidhī* ḥadīth no. 2516

Do not associate anyone with Allāh (in worship), even if you are killed and burned (because of this belief of *Tawḥīd*).[114] [Reported by Aḥmad]

Having *Īmān* in Destiny Is a Foundation Of *Īmān*

Anas ؓ narrated that the Messenger of Allāh ﷺ said:

Three things are from the basis of *Īmān*: To refrain from (killing) a person who utters: None has the right to be worshipped in truth except Allah, and not to declare them a disbeliever for committing a sin, and not to expel them from Islām due to any deed. *Jīhād* abides, since the day Allāh dispatched me (as a Prophet) until the last of my nation fight Dajjāl. *Jīhād* will not be invalidated by the tyranny of a tyrant nor the justice of one who is just. And, to have *Īmān* in the Divine Decree (destiny)."[115] [Reported by Abū Dāwūd]

That is, he must believe with certainty that the Divine Decree (destiny) is true.

'Abdullāh Bin 'Amr Bin al-'Āṣ ؓ narrated in *marfū'* form that the Messenger of Allāh ﷺ said:

Allāh decided the decrees of creation fifty thousand years before He created the Heavens and the Earth. He said: And His Throne was above the water.[116] [Reported by Muslim]

---

114 *Musnad Aḥmad* vol no.5 pg no.238, *Ṣaḥīḥ at-Targhīb Wat-Tarhīb* vol no.2 pg no.334. For details see *Irwā ul-Ghalīl* by al-Albānī vol no.8 pg no.89
115 *Sunan Abī Dāwūd* ḥadīth no.2532. This *Isnād* contains a narrator called Yazīd Bin Abī Nushbah who is unknown, therefore this narration is weak.
116 *Ṣaḥīḥ Muslim* ḥadīth no.2653

It is also narrated from Ibn 'Umar ﷺ that the Messenger of Allāh ﷺ said:

> Everything is decided and decreed, even incapability (foolishness) and ability (wisdom).[117] [Reported by Muslim]

That is, it is written in the destiny of people when they will be foolish and wise.

Ibn Mas'ūd ﷺ narrated in *marfū'* form that the Messenger of Allāh ﷺ said:

> One of you may do the deeds of the people of Paradise until there is a distance of one yard between him and Paradise, then the book (Decree) overtakes him and he does the deeds of the people of the Fire and enters it. And one of you may do the deeds of the people of the Fire until there is a distance of one yard between him and the Fire, then the book (Decree) overtakes him and he does the deeds of the people of Paradise, and enters it.[118] [Agreed upon]

The book (Decree) overtaking means that destiny prevails.

In the ḥadīth narrated by Sahl Bin Sa'd ﷺ the words are as follows:

> A man may do the deeds of [the people of] Paradise, or so it seems to the people, although he is one of the people of the Fire, and a man may do the deeds of [the people of] the Fire, or so it seems to the people, although he is one of the people of Paradise, for the end result is dependant and given according

117 *Ṣaḥīḥ Muslim* ḥadīth no.2655
118 *Ṣaḥīḥ al-Bukhārī* ḥadīth no.3036, *Ṣaḥīḥ Muslim* ḥadīth no.2643

to one's final deeds.[119] [Agreed upon]

That is, the end result is dependent on what actions are done at the final part of an individual's life, although this end result is written in the beginning (before being born into this world). Therefore, both fear and hope have been proven in this ḥadīth. This ḥadīth is also a proof of the Divine Decree and destiny similar to the other aḥādīth mentioned previously.

ʿĀʾīshah ﷺ narrated that the Messenger of Allāh ﷺ said:

> Allāh created people for Paradise, He created them for it when they were in their fathers' loins. And He created people for the Fire, He created them for it when they were in their fathers' loins.[120] [Reported by Muslim]

That is, everyone's destiny has been determined before he is born and every person ends their life in this world according to what is in their destiny.

In the ḥadīth narrated by ʿAlī ﷺ the Messenger of Allāh ﷺ said:

> Keep striving and doing deeds, for everyone will be helped to do that for which he was created.[121] [Agreed upon]

The ability to do good deeds becomes easy for him who is blessed, and the ability of bad deeds becomes easy for him who is not blessed.

This is a great sign in this world that shows if someone is from the people of Paradise or Hell in this world. Allāh says:

---

119 *Ṣaḥīḥ al-Bukhārī* ḥadīth no.6233, *Ṣaḥīḥ Muslim* ḥadīth no.112, 179
120 *Ṣaḥīḥ Muslim* ḥadīth no.2662
121 *Ṣaḥīḥ al-Bukhārī* ḥadīth no.4661, *Ṣaḥīḥ Muslim* ḥadīth no.2647

وَنَفْسٍ وَمَا سَوَّاهَا ۝٧ فَأَلْهَمَهَا فُجُورَهَا وَتَقْوَاهَا ۝٨

{And [by] the soul and He who proportioned it. And inspired it [with discernment of] its wickedness and its righteousness.} [Sūrah ash-Shams: 7-8]

Destiny Should Not Be Used as an Excuse for Justifying Evil Deeds

Adultery, theft, drunkenness and all sins and disobedience are all due to the will and destiny of Allāh, but the servant should not take destiny as an argument in such a place, rather he should attribute the sin towards himself. This is because although Allāh is the creator of the actions of the servants, the cause of them is the servant himself, therefore the sin should not be attributed to Allāh.

The following words are mentioned in a *dūʿā* narrated from the Prophet ﷺ: "And evil cannot be attributed to You."[122]

The One Who Denies the Divine Decree (Destiny) Is a Disbeliever

Whosoever denies destiny becomes a disbeliever.

Ibn ʿAbbās ؓ narrated a ḥadīth that the Messenger of Allāh ﷺ said:

> There are two groups in my Ummah for whom there is no share in Islam: The Murjiʿah and the Qadarīyah.[123] [Reported

122 *Ṣaḥīḥ Muslim* ḥadīth no.771

123 *Sunan at-Tirmidhī* ḥadīth no.2149. This *Isnād* contains a narrator called Nīzār who is unknown, therefore this narration is weak.

by at-Tirmidhī]

The Prophet ﷺ also said:

> Among my Ummah, those who deny the Divine Decree (destiny) will be transformed[124], disfigured and distorted.

It has been narrated by Ibn 'Umar ﷺ in *Sunans Abī Dāwūd* and *al-Tirmidhī*.[125]

In another narration the Prophet ﷺ said:

> Those who deny the Divine Decree (destiny) are the Zoroastrians of this Ummah. If they get sick, do not visit them, and if they die, do not attend (their funerals).[126] [Reported by Aḥmad and Abū Dāwūd]

'Alī ﷺ narrated in *marfū'* form that the Messenger of Allāh ﷺ said:

> An individual shall not have *Īmān* until he has *Īmān* in four (things): The testimony that there is no deity worthy of being worshipped in truth except Allāh, that I am the Messenger of Allāh ﷺ whom He sent with the Truth, he believes in the death, he believes in the Resurrection after death, and he believes in the Divine Decree (destiny).[127] [Reported by at-Tirmidhī and Ibn Mājah]

---

124 [TN] It is the transformation of the appearance of some humans, for example, into dogs or monkeys. Some said it is figurative, referring to a transformation and collapse of the hearts, but the first definition is more appropriate.
125 *Sunan Abī Dāwūd* ḥadīth no.4613, *Sunan at-Tirmidhī* ḥadīth no.2153
126 *Musnad Aḥmad* vol no.5 pg no.406, *Sunan Abī Dāwūd* ḥadīth no.4691
127 *Sunan at-Tirmidhī* ḥadīth no.2145, *Sunan Ibn Mājah* ḥadīth no.81

Allāh says:

آمَنَ الرَّسُولُ بِمَا أُنزِلَ إِلَيْهِ مِن رَّبِّهِ وَالْمُؤْمِنُونَ ۚ كُلٌّ آمَنَ بِاللَّهِ وَمَلَائِكَتِهِ
وَكُتُبِهِ وَرُسُلِهِ لَا نُفَرِّقُ بَيْنَ أَحَدٍ مِّن رُّسُلِهِ ۚ وَقَالُوا سَمِعْنَا وَأَطَعْنَا ۖ غُفْرَانَكَ
رَبَّنَا وَإِلَيْكَ الْمَصِيرُ ﴿٢٨٥﴾

{The Messenger has believed in what was revealed to him from his Rabb and [so have] the believers. All of them have believed in Allāh and His angels and His books and His messengers, [saying], "We make no distinction between any of His messengers." And they say, "We hear and we obey. [We seek] Your forgiveness, our Rabb, and to You is the [final] destination."} [Sūrah al-Baqarah: 285]

The subject of this *āyah* and the previously mentioned aḥādīth has been based on (the narration), "I believe in Allāh...etc."[128]

A person who possesses the previously mentioned attributes is a believer.

Allāh says:

وَلَا تَمُوتُنَّ إِلَّا وَأَنتُم مُّسْلِمُونَ ﴿١٠٢﴾

{And do not die except as Muslims [in submission to Him].} [Sūrah Āl-'Imrān: 102]

O My *Rabb*, you are my guardian in this world and in the hereafter. Make me die as a Muslim and join me with the righteous people

128 [TN] *Ṣaḥīḥ Muslim* ḥadīth no.38

only.

Date of Compilation

This treatise was completed in two days on Wednesday, the 9th of Jūmādul Ākhirah in the year 1305 Hijrī.

All complete praise is for Allāh alone first and foremost which I express externally and internally.